LEADERSHIP GOLD

LESSONS LEARNED *from a* LIFETIME *of* LEADING

———— ∽ ————

JOHN C. MAXWELL

THOMAS NELSON

Since 1798

NASHVILLE   DALLAS   MEXICO CITY   RIO DE JANEIRO   BEIJING

Published in Nashville, Tennessee, by Thomas Nelson. Thomas Nelson is a registered trademark of Thomas Nelson, Inc.

Published in association with Yates & Yates, www.yates2.com.

Thomas Nelson, Inc. titles may be purchased in bulk for educational, business, fund-raising, or sales promotional use. For information, please e-mail SpecialMarkets@ThomasNelson.com.

Library of Congress Cataloging-in-Publication Data

Maxwell, John C., 1947–
  Leadership gold : lessons learned from a lifetime of leading / John C. Maxwell.
    p. cm.
  Summary: "Learning to lead effectively"—Provided by publisher.
  Includes bibliographical references (p.   ).
  ISBN: 978-0-7852-1411-3 (hardcover)
  ISBN: 978-1-4002-8007-0 (IE)
  1. Leadership. 2. Industrial management. I. Title.
HD57.7.M39426 2007
658.4'092—dc22   2007036802

Printed in the United States of America
08 09 10 11 RRD 7 6

CONTENTS

CONTENTS

DEDICATION

Leadership Gold is dedicated to Ella Ashley Miller, our fourth grandchild. Her gentle nature continually draws us to her. We pray that as she grows older she will mine the "gold" out of the lessons of life.

ACKNOWLEDGMENTS

Thank you to
Charlie Wetzel, my writer
Stephanie Wetzel, who proofs and edits the manuscript
Linda Eggers, my assistant

SEARCHING FOR GOLD

I confess I've wanted to write this book for almost a decade. In a way, I've been working on it for most of my life. But I promised myself that I would not sit down and write it until I turned sixty. In February of 2007, I reached that milestone and began writing.

I've had a remarkable and rewarding journey as a leader. In 1964, at the age of seventeen, I started reading and filing thoughts on the subject of leadership, because I knew leading was going to be an important part of my career. At age twenty-two, I held my first leadership position. In 1976, I became convinced that everything rises and falls on leadership. That belief was accompanied by a passion to be a lifelong student and teacher of this vital subject.

Learning to lead effectively has been a real challenge. Teaching others to lead effectively has been an even greater one. During the late 1970s, I poured myself into training and raising up potential leaders. To my delight, I discovered that leaders could be developed. That eventually prompted me to write my first leadership book in 1992, entitled *Developing the Leader Within You*. Since then I have written many others. For more than thirty years, leading and teaching leadership have been my life's work.

ADDING VALUE TO YOUR LEADERSHIP

This book is a result of years of living in a leadership environment and learning through trial and error what it means to be a leader. The lessons I've learned are personal and often simple, yet they can have a profound impact. I have spent my entire life mining them. I think of each chapter as a gold nugget. In the hands of the right person, they can add tremendous value to their leadership.

As you read each chapter, please understand that . . .

1. I'm still learning about leadership. I haven't arrived, and this book is not my final answer on the subject of leadership. Within weeks of this book's publication, there will be thoughts I wish I could add. Why? Because I continue to learn and grow. I hope to keep growing until the day I die. I expect to keep discovering nuggets that I want to share with others.

2. Many people have contributed to the leadership gold in this book. One of the chapters in this book is entitled "Few Leaders Are Successful Unless a Lot of People Want Them to Be." That has certainly been true for me. It's said that a wise person learns from his mistakes. A wiser one learns from others' mistakes. But the wisest person of all learns from others' successes. Today I stand on the shoulders of many leaders who have added great value to my life. Tomorrow I hope *you* will be able to stand on *my* shoulders.

3. What I'm teaching can be learned by nearly anyone. Greek philosopher Plato said, "The greater part of instruction is being reminded of things you already know." That's what the best learning is. As an author and teacher, what I try to do is help people truly understand in a new and clear way something that they have long sensed intuitively. I try to create "aha moments."

Though I have lived my life in leadership by moving forward, I have begun to better understand it by looking backward. Now at age sixty, I want to share with you the most important lessons I've learned as a leader. This book is my attempt to take the leadership gold I've mined through painful trial and error and put it on the "lowest shelf" so that inexperienced as well as experienced leaders can have access to it. You don't have to be an expert to understand what I'm teaching, and you don't have to be a CEO to apply it. I never want anyone who reads my books to be like *Peanuts*' Charlie Brown, who admired a sand castle he had created on the beach only to have it leveled by a huge downpour. As he looked at the smooth place where his artwork had once stood, he said, "There must be a lesson here, but I don't know what it is." My goal isn't to impress you while knowledge and insight elude you. It's to be a friend who helps you.

4. Much of the leadership gold I'm sharing is a result of leadership mistakes I made. Some of the things I've learned were very painful to me at the time. I can still feel the sting as I pass them on to you. I am reminded of how often I have made mistakes. Yet I am also encouraged because I'm glad to recognize that I am wiser today than I was in years past.

Poet Archibald MacLeish remarked, "There's only one thing more painful than learning from experience, and that is not learning from experience." Too often I see people make a mistake and stubbornly plow ahead only to end up repeating the same mistake. With great resolve they say to themselves, "Try and try again!" How much better it would be to say, "Try, then stop, think, change, and then try again."

5. Your ability to become a better leader depends on how you respond. Reading a book is never enough to make a difference in your life. What has the potential to make you better is your response. Please don't take shortcuts with this book. Hammer every gold nugget into something useful that can help you become a better leader. Don't be like the boy playing chess with his grandfather, who cried, "Oh no! Not again! Grandpa, you always win!"

"What do you want me to do," replied the old man, "lose on purpose? You won't learn anything if I do that."

The boy responded, "I don't want to learn anything. I just want to win!"

Wanting to win isn't enough. You have to go through a process to improve. That takes patience, perseverance, and intentionality. William A. Ward said, "Committing a great truth to memory is admirable; committing it to life is wisdom."

I suggest that you keep this book as your companion for a significant amount of time so that it becomes a part of your life. Author and professor Peter Senge defines learning as "a process that occurs over time and always integrates thinking and doing." He goes on to say, "Learning is highly contextual. . . . It happens in the context of something meaningful and when the learner is taking action."

If you are an emerging leader, I recommend that you spend twenty-six weeks working your way through the book—one week for every chapter. Read the chapter and then follow the instructions in that chapter's application section. If you allow each lesson to sink in and then flesh it out by taking action before going on to the next one, I believe that in time you will be amazed by the positive changes that occur in your leadership. I've also created *Go for Gold*, a companion to *Leadership Gold* to help individuals gain further insight and learn additional skills related to each gold nugget. And you can also visit www.johnmaxwell.com/leadershipgold to see video clips, hear audio excerpts, and find other tools to help you learn more. Leadership development is a process, and anything you can do to reinforce what you're learning helps you to make it more permanent.

If you are a more experienced leader, take fifty-two weeks. Why longer? Because after you have worked your way through a chapter, you should spend a week taking people you are mentoring through that same chapter. By the end of the year, not only will you have grown, but you will have helped other emerging leaders to go to the next level! A Mentoring Moment is included after the application exercises to help you. Each has suggestions for helping people grow in leadership related to the area covered in the chapter. I recommend that you also ask anyone you mentor to use *Go for Gold*.

You will need to have achieved a degree of rapport and trust with people before being able to engage in some of the suggestions. If you don't have that with individuals you intend to mentor, invest time to build the relationship so that you can speak into their lives.

LEADERSHIP MAKES A DIFFERENCE

Why should you go through all this trouble to learn more about leadership? For that matter, why have I worked so hard to learn about leadership and mine gold nuggets for forty years? Because good leadership always makes a difference! I've seen what good leadership can do. I've seen it turn around organizations and positively impact the lives of thousands of individuals. True, leadership is not easy to learn, but what worthwhile thing is? Becoming a better leader pays dividends, but it takes great effort. Leadership requires a lot from a person. It is demanding and complex. Here's what I mean . . .

Leadership is the willingness to put oneself at risk.

Leadership is the passion to make a difference with others.

Leadership is being dissatisfied with the current reality.

Leadership is taking responsibility while others are making excuses.

Leadership is seeing the possibilities in a situation while others are seeing the limitations.

Leadership is the readiness to stand out in a crowd.

Leadership is an open mind and an open heart.

Leadership is the ability to submerge your ego for the sake of what is best.

Leadership is evoking in others the capacity to dream.

Leadership is inspiring others with a vision of what they can contribute.

Leadership is the power of one harnessing the power of many.

Leadership is your heart speaking to the hearts of others.

Leadership is the integration of heart, head, and soul.

Leadership is the capacity to care, and in caring, to liberate the ideas, energy, and capacities of others.

Leadership is the dream made reality.

Leadership is, above all, courageous.

If these leadership thoughts quicken your pulse and stir your heart, then learning more about leadership will make a difference in you, and you will make a difference in the lives of others. Turn the page, and let's get started.

1

IF IT'S LONELY AT THE TOP, YOU'RE NOT DOING SOMETHING RIGHT

My father's generation believed that leaders should never get too close to the people they lead. "Keep a distance" was a phrase I often heard. Good leaders were supposed to be a little above and apart from those they led. As a result, when I began my leadership journey, I made sure to keep some distance between me and my people. I tried to be close enough to lead them, but far enough away to not be influenced by them.

This balancing act immediately created a lot of inner conflict for me. Honestly, I liked being close to the people I led. Plus, I felt that one of my strengths was my ability to connect with people. Both of these factors caused me to fight the instruction I had received to keep a distance. And sure enough, within a few months of accepting my first leadership position, my wife, Margaret, and I began developing close friendships. We were enjoying our work and the people in the organization.

Like many leaders early in their career, I knew that I would not stay in this first job forever. It was a good experience, but I was soon ready for bigger challenges. After three years, I resigned to accept a position in Lancaster, Ohio. I'll never forget the response of most people when they realized we were leaving: "How could you do this after all we have done together?" Many people took my departure personally. I could see they felt hurt. That really bothered me. Instantly, the words of older leaders rang in my ears: "Don't get too close to your people." As I left that assignment to take my next leadership position, I promised myself to keep people from getting too close to me.

THIS TIME IT'S PERSONAL

In my second position, for the first time in my leadership journey, I could employ staff to help me. One young man showed great promise, so I hired him and began pouring my life into him. I soon discovered that training and developing people was both a strength and a joy.

This staff member and I did everything together. One of the best ways to train others is to let them accompany you to observe what you do, give some training, and then let them make an attempt at doing it. That's what we did. It was my first experience in mentoring.

I thought everything was going great. Then one day I found out that he had taken some sensitive information I had shared with him and violated my confidence by telling others about it. It not only hurt me as a leader, but it also hurt me personally. I felt betrayed. Needless to say, I let him go. And once again, the words of more experienced leaders rang in my ears: "Don't get too close to your people."

> *Loneliness is not a positional issue; it is a personality issue.*

This time I had learned my lesson. I once again determined to keep space between me and everyone around me. I would hire staff to do their jobs. And I would do my job. And we would only get together at the annual Christmas party!

For six months I managed to maintain this professional separation. But then one day I realized that keeping everyone at a distance was a double-edged sword. The good news was that if I kept people at a distance, nobody would ever hurt me. But the bad news was that no one would ever be able to help me either. So at age twenty-five, I made a decision: As a leader, I would "walk slowly through the crowd." I would take the time—and the risk—of getting close to people and letting them get close to me. I would vow to love people before trying to lead them. This choice would at times make me vulnerable. I would get hurt. Yet the close relationships would allow me to help them as well as be helped by them. That decision has changed my life and my leadership.

LONELINESS IS NOT A LEADERSHIP ISSUE

There's a cartoon in which an executive is shown sitting forlornly behind a huge desk. Standing meekly on the other side of the desk is a man dressed in work clothes, who says, "If it's any comfort to you, it's lonely at the bottom too." Being at the top doesn't mean you have to be lonely. Neither does being at the bottom. I've met lonely people at the bottom, on the top, and in the middle. I now realize that loneliness is not a positional issue; it is a personality issue.

To many people, the leader's image is that of an individual standing alone at the top of the mountain, looking down on his people. He's separated, isolated, and lonely. Thus the saying "It's lonely at the top." But I would argue that the phrase was never made by a great leader. If you are leading others and you're lonely, then you're not doing it right. Think about it. If you're all alone, that means nobody is following you. And if nobody is following you, you're not really leading!

Taking people to the top is what good leaders do.

What kind of a leader would leave everyone behind and take the journey alone? A selfish one. Taking people to the top is what good leaders do. Lifting people to a new level is a requirement for effective leadership. That's hard to do if you get too far from your people— because you can no longer sense their needs, know their dreams, or feel their heartbeat. Besides, if things aren't getting better for people as a result of their leader's efforts, then they need a different leader.

TRUTHS ABOUT THE TOP

Because this leadership issue has been so personal to me, I've given it a lot of thought over the years. Here are some things you need to know:

No One Ever Got to the Top Alone

Few leaders are successful unless a lot of people want them to be. No leaders are successful without a few people helping them. Sadly, as soon as some leaders arrive at the top, they spend their time trying to push others off the top. They play king of the hill because of their insecurity or competitiveness. That may work for a time, but it usually won't last long. When your goal is to knock others down, you spend too much of your time and energy watching out for people who would do the same to you. Instead, why not give others a hand up and ask them to join you?

Making It to the Top Is Essential to Taking Others to the Top

There are a lot of people in the world who are willing to give advice on things they've never experienced. They are like bad travel agents: they sell you an expensive ticket and say, "I hope you enjoy the trip." Then you never see them again. In contrast, good leaders are like tour guides. They know the territory because they've made the trip before, and they do what they can to make the trip enjoyable and successful for everybody.

> *A leader's credibility begins with personal success. It ends with helping others achieve personal success.*

A leader's credibility begins with personal success. It ends with helping others achieve personal success. To gain credibility, you must consistently demonstrate three things:

1. Initiative: You have to *get up* to go up.
2. Sacrifice: You have to *give up* to go up.
3. Maturity: You have to *grow up* to go up.

If you show the way, people will want to follow you. The higher you go, the greater the number of people who will be willing to travel with you.

Taking People to the Top Is More Fulfilling Than Arriving Alone

A few years ago I had the privilege of speaking on the same stage as Jim Whittaker, the first American to climb Mount Everest. During lunch I asked him what had given him the most fulfillment as a mountain climber. His answer surprised me.

"I have helped more people get to the top of Mount Everest than any other person," he replied. "Taking people to the top who could never get there without my assistance is my greatest accomplishment."

Evidently this is a common way of thinking for great mountain guides. Years ago I saw an interview with a guide on *60 Minutes*. People had died while attempting to climb Mount Everest, and a surviving guide was asked, "Would the guides have died if they were not taking others with them to the top?"

"No," he answered, "but the purpose of the guide is to take people to the top."

Then the interviewer asked, "Why do mountain climbers risk their lives to climb mountains?"

The guide responded, "It is obvious that you have never been to the top of the mountain."

I remember thinking to myself that mountain guides and leaders have a lot in common. There is a big difference between a *boss* and a *leader*. A boss says, "Go." A leader says, "Let's go." The purpose of leadership is to take others to the top. And when you take others who might not make it to the top otherwise, there's no other feeling like it in the world. To those who have never had the experience, you can't explain it. To those who have, you don't need to.

Much of the Time Leaders Are Not at the Top

Leaders rarely remain stationary. They are constantly on the move. Sometimes they are going down the mountain to find new potential leaders. At other times they are trying to make the climb with a group of people. The best ones spend much of their time serving other leaders and lifting them up.

Jules Ormont said, "A great leader never sets himself above his followers except in carrying responsibilities." Good leaders who remain connected with their people stoop—that's the only way to reach down and pull others up. If you want to be the best leader you can be, don't allow insecurity, pettiness, or jealousy to keep you from reaching out to others.

ADVICE TO LONELY LEADERS

If you find yourself too far from your people—either by accident or by design—then you need to change. True, there will be risks. You may hurt others or be hurt yourself. But if you want to be the most effective leader you can be, there is no viable alternative. Here's how to get started:

1. Avoid Positional Thinking

Leadership is relational as much as it is positional. An individual who takes a relational approach to leadership will never be lonely. The time spent in building relationships creates friendships with others. Positional leaders, on the other hand, are often lonely. Every time they use their title and permission to "persuade" their people to do something, they create distance between themselves and others. They are essentially saying, "I'm up here; you're down there. So do what I say." That makes people feel small, alienates them, and drives a wedge between them and the leader. Good leaders don't belittle people—they enlarge them.

> *Leadership is relational as much as it is positional. An individual who takes a relational approach to leadership will never be lonely.*

Every year I invest time teaching leadership internationally. Positional leadership is a way of life in many developing countries. Leaders gather and protect power. They alone are allowed to be on top, and everyone else is expected to follow. Sadly, this practice keeps potential leaders from developing and creates loneliness for the one who leads.

If you are in a leadership position, do not rely on your title to convince people to follow you. Build relationships. Win people over. Do that and you will never be a lonely leader.

2. Realize the Downsides of Success and Failure

Success can be dangerous—and so can failure. Anytime you think of yourself as "a success," you start to separate yourself from others you view as less successful. You start to think, *I don't need to see them,* and you withdraw. Ironically, failure also leads to withdrawal, but for other reasons. If you think of yourself as "a failure," you avoid others, thinking, *I don't want to see them.* Both extremes in thinking can create an unhealthy separation from others.

3. Understand That You Are in the People Business

The best leaders know that leading people requires loving them! I've never met a good leader who didn't care about people. Ineffective leaders have the wrong attitude, saying, "I love mankind. It's the people I can't stand." But good leaders understand that people do not care how much you know until they know how much you care. You must like people or you will never add value to them. And if you become indifferent to people, you may be only a few steps away from manipulating them. No leader should ever do that.

4. Buy Into the Law of Significance

The Law of Significance in *The 17 Indispensible Laws of Teamwork* states, "One is too small a number to achieve greatness." No accomplishment of real value has ever been achieved by a human being working alone. I challenge you to think of one. (I've made this challenge at conferences for years and no one has succeeded in identifying one yet!) Honestly, if on your own you can fulfill the vision you have for your life and work, then you're aiming too low. Occasionally a person will introduce himself to me by saying, "I am a self-made man." I am often tempted to reply, "I'm so sorry. If you've made everything yourself, you haven't made much."

In my organizations I don't have employees; I have teammates. Yes, I do pay people and offer them benefits. But people don't work for me. They work with me. We are working together to fulfill the vision. Without them, I cannot succeed. Without me, they cannot succeed. We're a team. We reach our goals together. We need each other. If we didn't, then one of us is in the wrong place.

~≈~

People working together for a common vision can be an incredible experience. Years ago when operatic tenors Jose Carreras, Placido Domingo, and Luciano Pavarotti were performing together, a reporter tried to find out if there was a competitive spirit among them.

Each singer was a superstar, and the reporter was hoping to uncover a rivalry between them. Domingo dismissed it. "You have to put all of your concentration into opening your heart to the music," he said. "You can't be rivals when you're together making music."

For many years now I have tried to maintain that kind of attitude toward the people I work with. Our focus is on what we are trying to accomplish together, not on hierarchies or professional distance or the preservation of power. I've come a long way from where I started in my leadership journey. In the beginning my attitude was that it was lonely at the top. But it has changed, following a progression that looks something like this:

"It's lonely at the top," to
"If it's lonely at the top, I must be doing something wrong," to
"Come up to the top and join me," to
"Let's go to the top together," to
"It's not lonely at the top."

Nowadays I never "climb the mountain" alone. My job is to make sure the team makes it to the top together. Some of the people I invite to go along pass me and climb higher than I do. That doesn't bother me. If I know I was able to give them a hand and pull them up along the way, then I feel very fulfilled. Sometimes they return the favor and pull me up to their level. I'm grateful for that too.

If you're a leader and you feel isolated, then you're not doing something right. Loneliness on the part of a leader is a choice. I choose to take the journey with people. I hope you do too.

APPLICATION EXERCISES

1. Are you better at the science or art of leadership? Some leaders are better at the technical side of leading: strategy, planning, finances, etc. Others are better at the people part: connecting, communicating, casting vision, motivating, etc. Which is your strength?

If you are more of a technical person, never lose sight of the fact that leadership is a people business. Take steps to improve your people skills. Try walking slowly through the halls so that you can talk to people and get to know them better. Read books or take courses. Ask a friend who is good with people to give you some tips. Seek counseling. Do whatever it takes to improve.

2. Why do you want to be at the top? Most people have a natural desire to improve their lives. For many, that means climbing the career ladder so that they can gain a higher position. If your only motivation for leading is career advancement and professional improvement, you are in danger of becoming the kind of positional leader who plays king of the hill with colleagues and employees. Spend some time soul searching to discover how your leadership can and should benefit others.

3. How big is your dream? What is your dream? What would you love to accomplish in your life and career? If it's something you can accomplish alone, you are missing your leadership potential. Anything worth doing is worth doing with others. Dream big. What can you imagine accomplishing that would require more than you can do on your own? What kinds of teammates would you need to accomplish it? How might the trip benefit them as well as you or the organization? Broaden your thinking and you will be more likely to think of climbing the summit with a team.

MENTORING MOMENT

As a leadership mentor, it is your job to assess how the people you are mentoring are handling relationships. Some people are limited by their inability to interact well with others. If they are disconnected with people above, beside, or below them in the organization's hierarchy, make it your goal to coach them in this area and to help them connect.

2

THE TOUGHEST PERSON TO LEAD IS ALWAYS YOURSELF

During a Q&A session at a conference, someone asked, "What has been your greatest challenge as a leader?" I think my response surprised nearly everyone in the auditorium.

"Leading me!" I answered. "That's always been my greatest challenge as a leader."

I think that's true for all leaders regardless of who they lead and what they accomplish. We sometimes think about accomplished leaders from history and assume that they had it all together. But if we really examine their lives, whether we're looking at King David, George Washington, or Winston Churchill, we'll see that they struggled to lead themselves well. That's why I say that the toughest person to lead is always yourself. It's like Walt Kelly exclaimed in his *Pogo* cartoon strip: "We have met the enemy and he is us."[1]

Acknowledging that leading myself is a challenge brings back some painful memories. Many of my leadership breakdowns have been personal breakdowns. In a leadership career that has spanned almost four decades, I've made plenty of mistakes, but I have experienced only four major leadership crises. And I'm sorry to say that all of them were my fault.

The first occurred in 1970, just two years into my first official leadership position. After two years of work, I had won over many people and there was a lot going on. However, one day I realized that my organization had no direction. Why? Because I lacked the ability to prioritize correctly and bring focus to my leadership. As a young leader, I didn't yet understand that activity does not necessarily equal accomplishment. As a result, my people, following my example, were wandering in the wilderness for sixteen months. In the end, I didn't really lead them anywhere.

The next crisis came in 1979. At that time I felt pulled in two directions. I had been successful in my second leadership position, but I also realized that if I was going to reach a broader audience, which I felt was the right thing to try to do, I would have to leave the organization I had been a part of for the first twelve years of my career. My uncertainty and the personal changes that I was dealing with negatively impacted the organization I led. I became unfocused, and my vision for the organization became cloudy. My passion and energy also began to wane. Leaders who aren't focused aren't as effective as they could be. As a result, we weren't moving forward as effectively as we could.

> *Human nature seems to endow us with the ability to size up everybody in the world except ourselves.*

The third occurred in 1991 when I was overloaded with work and my life was out of balance. Because I had been leading my organization successfully for ten years, I thought I could take a few shortcuts to make things easier for me. I made three difficult decisions in rapid succession without doing proper due diligence or taking the time needed to process everyone through them. What a mistake! As a result, the people were not prepared for the decisions—and I was unprepared for their response. The trust that it had taken me ten years to build began to erode. To make matters worse, when the people who questioned my decisions balked at following my lead, I became increasingly impatient. I angrily thought, *What is their problem? Why don't they "get it" and get on with it?* Within a few weeks, I realized that the problem wasn't them. It was me. I ended up having to apologize to everyone for my attitude.

The fourth occurred in 2001 and involved a staff member whom I needed to let go. I'll tell you more about that in "A Leader's First Responsibility Is to Define Reality." The bottom line was that my unwillingness to make difficult decisions cost me many dollars and some key personnel. Once again, I was the source of the problem.

JUDGE FOR YOURSELF

If we are honest with ourselves, we'll admit that the toughest person to lead is ourselves. Most people don't need to worry about the competition. Other people aren't the reason they lose. If they don't win, it's because they disqualify themselves.

That's as true for leaders as it is for anyone else. They are often their own worst enemies. Why is that?

We Don't See Ourselves as We See Others

My years counseling others taught me something important: people seldom see themselves realistically. Human nature seems to endow us with the ability to size up everybody in the world except ourselves. That's why in my book *Winning with People* I start with the Mirror Principle, which advises, "The First Person We Must Examine Is Ourselves." If you don't look at yourself realistically, you will never understand where your personal difficulties lie. And if you can't see them, you won't be able to lead yourself effectively.

We Are Harder on Others Than We Are on Ourselves

Most people use two totally different sets of criteria for judging themselves versus others. We tend to judge others according to their *actions*. It's very cut-and-dried. However, we judge ourselves by our *intentions*. Even if we do the wrong thing, if we believe our motives were good, we let ourselves off the hook. And we are often willing to do that over and over before requiring ourselves to change.

KEYS TO LEADING YOURSELF

The truth is that to be successful in any endeavor, we need to learn how to get out of our own way. That's as true for leaders as it is for anyone else.

Because I have known for many years that the toughest person to lead is me, I have taken steps to help me do that. By practicing the following four things, I have tried to lead myself well as a prerequisite to leading others:

1. Learn Followership

Bishop Fulton J. Sheen remarked, "Civilization is always in danger when those who have never learned to obey are given the right to command." Only a leader who has followed well knows how to lead others well. Good leadership requires an understanding of the world that followers live in. Connecting with your people becomes possible because you have walked in their shoes. You know what it means to be under authority and thus have a better sense of how authority should be exercised. In contrast, leaders who have never followed well or submitted to authority tend to be prideful, unrealistic, rigid, and autocratic.

> *"Civilization is always in danger when those who have never learned to obey are given the right to command."*
> —*Bishop Fulton J. Sheen*

If those words describe your leadership, you need to do some soul searching. Arrogant leaders are rarely effective in the long run. They alienate their followers, their colleagues, and their leaders. Learn to submit to another person's leadership and to follow well, and you will become a more humble—and effective—leader.

2. Develop Self-Discipline

It's said that one day Frederick the Great of Prussia was walking on the outskirts of Berlin when he encountered a very old man walking ramrod straight in the opposite direction.

"Who are you?" Frederick asked his subject.

"I am a king," replied the old man.

"A king!" laughed Frederick. "Over what kingdom do you reign?"

"Over myself," was the proud old man's reply.

Each of us is "monarch" of our own lives. We are responsible for ruling our actions and decisions. To make consistently good decisions, to take the right action when needed, and to refrain from the wrong actions requires character and self-discipline. To do otherwise is to lose control of ourselves—

to do or say things we regret, to miss opportunities we are given, to spend ourselves into debt. As King Solomon remarked, "The rich rule over the poor, and the borrower is servant to the lender."[2]

In "Decision of Character," British essayist John Foster writes, "A man without decision of character can never be said to belong to himself. He belongs to whatever can make a captive of him." When we are foolish, we want to conquer the world. When we are wise, we want to conquer ourselves. That begins when we do what we should no matter how we feel about it.

3. Practice Patience

The leaders I know tend to be impatient. They look ahead, think ahead, and want to move ahead. And that can be good. Being one step ahead makes you a leader. However, that can also be bad. Being fifty steps ahead could make you a martyr.

Few worthwhile things in life come quickly. There is no such thing as instant greatness or instant maturity. We are used to instant oatmeal, instant coffee, and microwave popcorn. But becoming a leader doesn't happen overnight. Microwave leaders don't have any staying power. Leadership is more of a Crock-Pot proposition. It takes time, but the end product is worth the wait.

> *When we are foolish, we want to conquer the world. When we are wise, we want to conquer ourselves.*

Leaders need to remember that the point of leading is not to cross the finish line first. It's to take people across the finish line with you. For that reason, leaders must deliberately slow their pace, stay connected to their people, enlist others to help fulfill the vision, and keep people going. You can't do that if you're running too far ahead of your people.

4. Seek Accountability

People who lead themselves well know a secret: they can't trust themselves. Good leaders know that power can be seductive, and they understand their own fallibility. To be a leader and deny this is to put yourself in danger.

Over the years, I've read about many leaders who failed ethically in their leadership. Can you guess what they had in common? They all thought it could never happen to them. There was a false sense of security. They thought they were incapable of ruining their lives and the lives of others.

Learning that was very sobering to me, because I shared the same attitude. I thought I was above such possibilities, and that scared me. At that moment, I made two decisions: First, I will not trust myself. Second, I will become accountable to someone other than myself. I believe those decisions have helped to keep me on track and able to lead myself and others.

Lack of accountability in our personal life will certainly lead to problems in our public life. We saw that time and time again with high-profile CEOs a few years ago. A Chinese proverb says, "When you see a good man, think of emulating him; when you see a bad man, examine your heart."

> "When you see a good man, think of emulating him; when you see a bad man, examine your heart."
> —Chinese proverb

Many people feel that accountability is a willingness to explain your actions. I believe that effective accountability begins way before we take action. It starts with getting advice from others. For leaders especially, this often develops in stages:

We don't want advice.
We don't object to advice.
We welcome advice.
We actively seek advice.
We often follow the advice given to us.

The willingness to seek and accept advice is a great indicator of accountability. If you seek it early—before you take action—you will be less likely to get off track. Most wrong actions come about because people are not being held accountable early enough.

Leading yourself well means that you hold yourself to a higher standard of accountability than others do. Why? Because you are held responsible not only for your own actions, but also for those of the people you lead. Leadership is a trust, not a right. For that reason, we must "fix" ourselves earlier than others may be required to. We must always seek to do what's right, no matter how high we rise or how powerful we become. It's a struggle we never outgrow. When Harry Truman was thrust into the presidency upon the death of Franklin Roosevelt, Sam Rayburn gave him some fatherly advice: "From here on out you're going to have lots of people around you. They'll try to put a wall around you and cut you off from any ideas but theirs. They'll tell you what a great man you are, Harry. But you and I both know you ain't."

> *"Nothing so conclusively proves a man's ability to lead others, as what he does from day to day to lead himself."*
> *—Thomas J. Watson*

Yesterday I participated in a conference call with board members of an organization who had to step in and hold a leader accountable for wrong actions he had taken. It was a sad experience. He will probably lose his leadership position. He has already lost their respect. If he had only led himself effectively first, the board's actions would not have been necessary. After the call I thought to myself, *When the leader doesn't inspect himself, the people don't respect him.*

Thomas J. Watson, the former chairman of IBM, said, "Nothing so conclusively proves a man's ability to lead others, as what he does from day to day to lead himself." How true. The smallest crowd you will ever lead is you—but it's the most important one. If you do that well, then you will earn the right to lead even bigger crowds.

To see a video clip of John Maxwell teaching more on this leadership principle and to access additional helpful tools and information, visit www.johnmaxwell.com/leadershipgold.

APPLICATION EXERCISES

1. How clearly do you see yourself? To get a more objective look at yourself, review your performance from the last year. List all of your major goals and objectives and then mark each as either "achieved" or "not achieved." Now talk to someone you know and respect and tell them you are evaluating a candidate for a job, and show them the list. Ask them what they think based on the "candidate's" achievements and failures. How does that person's evaluation jibe with your own?

2. Where do you need to grow? In which of the following areas do you most need to grow: self-discipline, "followership," or patience? What new task or practice can you take on to develop it? Maybe you should set a recreational goal that will require at least a year's work, or put off buying something you've wanted for a long time. Perhaps you should offer to do a task for a leader whom you find difficult to follow. Or you could consider volunteering; it requires patience, followership, and self-discipline.

3. How well do you take advice? Ask five to ten friends, colleagues, and family members to evaluate you using the levels mentioned in the chapter. Each of the following is worth the number beside it:

1. You don't want advice.
2. You don't object to advice.
3. You welcome advice.
4. You actively seek advice.
5. You often follow the advice given to you.

Average their scores. If your average is below a 4, you need to improve in this area. Begin enlisting others in your information-gathering process before you make decisions. If you are married, begin with your spouse.

MENTORING MOMENT

Have a very frank conversation with each of the people you mentor explaining how they're doing when it comes to leading themselves. Provide specific examples to illustrate your point of view. Then assist those who need to grow in this area by giving them assignments that will help them show initiative and become more responsible. Meet with them periodically to provide accountability in this area.

3

≈

DEFINING MOMENTS DEFINE YOUR LEADERSHIP

One of the leaders I admire most is Winston Churchill, England's prime minister who stood up against the Nazis during World War II. He was a leader's leader! He once remarked, "In every age there comes a time when a leader must come forward to meet the needs of the hour. Therefore, there is no potential leader who does not have an opportunity to make a positive difference in society. Tragically, there are times when a leader does not rise to the hour."

What determines whether a leader emerges to meet the challenge of the hour? More to the point, what will determine whether *you* will step forward to successfully meet the challenges *you* face? I believe the determining factor is how you handle certain critical moments in your life. These moments will define who you are as a person and as a leader.

HOW WILL YOU BE DEFINED?

If you are familiar with my philosophy of leadership and my teaching on success, then you know that I'm a big believer in personal growth. I don't believe in overnight successes. In fact, one of my core principles is the Law of Process in my book *The 21 Irrefutable Laws of Leadership*. It states, "Leadership develops daily, not in a day." However, I also believe that the choices we make in critical moments help to form us and to inform others about who we are. They are defining moments, and here's why I think they are important:

1. Defining Moments Show Us Who We Really Are

Most days in our lives come and go; they are much like all the others and don't stand out. But there are a few days that are unlike all the others. They do stand out because they give us an opportunity to stand up, be set apart from the rest of the crowd, and seize that moment—or to remain sitting with the rest of the crowd and let it pass. These moments—for better or worse—define us. They show us what we are really made of.

> *The choices we make in critical moments help to form us and to inform others about who we are.*

We often focus on the milestones of life, the important events that mark seasons and accomplishments. We happily anticipate a graduation, wedding, or promotion. But some of our defining moments come as a total surprise, often appearing during times of crisis:

- Facing a personal failure
- Taking a stand on an issue
- Experiencing suffering
- Being asked to forgive
- Making an unpleasant choice

Sometimes we can sense the importance of our actions in the moment. We can see two clear paths ahead of us, one leading up, the other down. Other times, sadly, our defining moments occur and we don't see them for what they are. Only afterward, when time has passed and we look back, do we understand their importance. Either way, they define who we are.

2. Defining Moments Declare to Others Who We Are

Most days we can wear masks and hide who we are from the people around us. During defining moments, we can't do that. Our résumés mean nothing. It doesn't matter how we have marketed ourselves. Our image means nothing. Defining moments put the spotlight on us. We have no time to put a spin on our actions. Whatever is truly inside us is revealed to everyone. Our character isn't made during these times—it is displayed!

For leaders, defining moments tell the people following them many of the things they really want to know: who their leaders are, what they stand for, and why they are leading. Handled well, a defining moment can cement a relationship and bond leaders and followers for life. Handled poorly, a defining moment can cost a leader his credibility and end his ability to lead.

Defining moments put the spotlight on us. . . . Our character isn't made during these times—it is displayed!

In the revised tenth anniversary edition of *The 21 Irrefutable Laws of Leadership*, I wrote about two defining moments in the leadership of President George W. Bush. His first term in office was defined by his response to the September 11 terrorist attacks. He connected with the hearts of the American people, and even people who hadn't voted for him were willing to give his leadership a chance. However, his second term of office was defined by his poor response to Katrina. It took only a few days for the people of the United States to feel the leadership vacuum—and even for many of the president's supporters to disapprove of his leadership.

My intention is not to be critical. All of us have experienced failure. My point is that the defining moments of leaders can have a dramatic effect on others. When leaders respond correctly, everyone wins. When they respond incorrectly, everyone loses.

3. Defining Moments Determine Who We Will Become

You will never be the same person after a defining moment. Somehow you will be moved. It may be forward, or it may be backward, but make no mistake—you will be moved. Why is that? Because defining moments are not normal, and what's "normal" doesn't work in those times.

I think of defining moments as intersections in our lives. They give us an opportunity to turn, change direction, and seek a new destination. They present options and opportunities. In these moments, we *must* choose.

And the choice we make will define us! What will we do? Our response puts us on a new path, and that new path will define who we will become in the future. After a defining moment, we will never be the same person again.

MOMENTS THAT DEFINED ME

The defining moments of my life have determined who I have become. Take away even one of them—good or bad—and I would not be the same person. And the defining moments that lie before me will continue to shape me.

As I look back at the many defining moments in my life and reflect on them, I can see that all of them fall into four categories:

Some Defining Moments Were Ground Breakers

Many of the defining moments of my life allowed me to start something new. More than twenty years ago, I was teaching leadership to a small group of people in Jackson, Mississippi. At the close of the seminar, one of the participants asked if it was possible to receive ongoing leadership training from me. I wasn't sure how that could be done. However, as we talked, I could sense that many of the other attendees desired the same thing.

In that moment, I made a quick decision. I told them that if they would be willing to pay a modest fee, I would promise to write and record a new one-hour leadership lesson every month and send it to them. I had never done anything like that before, and I wasn't even sure how to do it, but I passed a sheet of paper around the room, and to my surprise, nearly every person signed up. At the end of

Defining moments are intersections that give us an opportunity to turn, change direction, and seek a new destination.

that day, I didn't recognize that I had experienced a defining moment, but I had. My promise to them turned into what I called a tape club—a leadership lesson subscription service on tape (and eventually CD) that rose to more than twenty thousand subscribers and continues even today.

Now more than two decades later, I can say with great assurance that my response in that moment was one of the most important leadership decisions I ever made. At the time, it looked like a lot of work. And it has been. But those monthly lessons allowed me to be a leadership mentor to thousands of leaders across the country and eventually around the world. Those lessons have provided material for many of the books I have written. And those lessons became the catalyst for me to start a resource company to facilitate the growth of leaders. Without that decision, the entire course of my life would have been different.

Some Defining Moments Were Heart Breakers

Not all defining moments are positive. I have experienced some very difficult moments, but sometimes those experiences have given me the opportunity to stop and make needed changes in my life. One such instance occurred on December 18, 1998. As our company Christmas party came to an end, I suddenly felt a debilitating pain and weight on my chest. It was a heart attack. As I lay on the floor waiting for an ambulance, reality hit me. My priorities were out of whack, and I wasn't nearly as healthy as I thought!

Over the next few weeks, I spent a lot of time reflecting on my health. I was working too hard. I wasn't taking enough time off with my family. I wasn't exercising regularly. And I wasn't eating the right food. The bottom line: my life was out of balance.

During this season, I learned a lesson that is best described by the words of Brian Dyson, former vice chairman and COO of Coca-Cola, who delivered the commencement address at Georgia Tech in 1996. In it, he explained this:

> Imagine life as a game in which you are juggling some five balls in the air. You name them—work, family, health, friends and spirit and you're keeping all of these in the air. You will soon understand that work is a rubber ball. If you drop it, it will bounce back. But the other four balls—family, health, friends and spirit are made of glass. If you drop one of these, they will be irrevocably scuffed, marked, nicked, damaged or even shattered. They will never be the same. You must understand that and strive for balance in your life.[1]

I was very fortunate. When I dropped the health ball, it got scuffed but it didn't shatter. Since receiving a second chance, I have redefined my priorities. I spend more time with my family. I exercise regularly. I try to eat right. I don't do these things perfectly, but I'm striving to live a more balanced life. I don't know what kinds of "balls" you may be juggling, but I recommend that you not wait until one of the important ones falls before examining your life. You can make changes without having to experience a heart breaker.

Some Defining Moments Were Cloud Breakers

Occasionally a defining moment comes as the result of seeing a new opportunity and taking action to seize it. That was the case for me several years ago. During the twenty-five years I worked as a pastor, I spent seventeen of them buying land, constructing buildings, and raising funds to pay for it.

One day a pastor and a key businessperson flew over to San Diego from Phoenix to have lunch with me. They were in a building program and said they came because I had a lot of experience raising the finances to make a vision a reality—something that isn't taught in seminary. At the close of our lunch, they asked me if I would help them raise the money for their building program. "If you can do this for your congregation," one of them said, "you can certainly help us."

At that moment, it was very clear to me. I could help them. And I should. Before they left, we shook hands and I agreed to help them. I went out to my car in the parking lot, called a friend, and said, "Next week we will begin helping churches raise money to realize their dreams." That was the birth of my company INJOY Stewardship Services.

Some Defining Moments Were Chart Breakers

The finest defining moments allow a person to soar to a much higher level. That was the case a few years ago at EQUIP, a nonprofit organization that my brother, Larry, and I founded in 1996 to train and resource leaders internationally. The first few years EQUIP was in existence were typical of a fledgling organization. We were trying to establish ourselves, engage donors to help us, and develop a team to lead this venture. Those years were filled with trial and error, adjustments and changes as we worked to establish credibility as a leadership organization.

As time went by, I could sense that EQUIP needed a vision that would capture the hearts and hands of those who believed in our mission. I discovered that vision and then presented it one evening at a banquet with hundreds of supporters of EQUIP. I painted a picture in which EQUIP would train and resource one million leaders around the world in five years, and I challenged them to help fulfill it. The vision connected with the people, and EQUIP soared to a new level. That night was a defining moment for hundreds of people that over five years became a life-changing experience for a million people.

> *Leaders become better leaders when they experience a defining moment and respond to it correctly.*

DEFINING YOUR MOMENTS

Leaders become better leaders when they experience a defining moment and respond to it correctly. Anytime they experience a breakthrough, it allows the people who follow them to also benefit. The difficulty with defining moments is that you don't get to choose them. You can't sit down with your calendar and say, "I'm going to schedule a defining moment for next Tuesday at eight o'clock." You cannot control when they will come. However, you can choose how you will handle them when they come, and you can take steps to prepare for them. Here's how:

1. Reflect on Defining Moments from the Past

It's said that those who do not study history are destined to repeat its mistakes. That statement applies not only in a broad sense to a nation or culture but also to individuals and their personal histories. The best teacher for a leader is evaluated experience. To predict how you will handle defining moments in the future, look at the ones from your past.

2. Prepare for Defining Moments in the Future

One of the most valuable things I've done in my life is to make major choices *before* times of crisis or decision. That has enabled me to simply *manage* those decisions in critical moments of my life. A few of these decisions I made as a teenager, many in my twenties and thirties, and a few later in life. I wrote about these decisions in depth in my book *Today Matters*, but I'll give them to you here so that you can get the gist:

Attitude: I will choose and display the right attitudes daily.
Priorities: I will determine and act upon important priorities daily.
Health: I will know and follow healthy guidelines daily.
Family: I will communicate with and care for my family daily.
Thinking: I will practice and develop good thinking daily.
Commitment: I will make and keep proper commitments daily.
Finances: I will earn and properly manage finances daily.
Faith: I will deepen and live out my faith daily.
Relationships: I will initiate and invest in solid relationships daily.
Generosity: I will plan for and model generosity daily.
Values: I will embrace and practice good values daily.
Growth: I will desire and experience improvements daily.

I don't have to wrestle with these issues during a defining moment. They are already settled, and I am free to focus on the situation at hand and make decisions based on them.

3. Make the Most of Defining Moments in the Present

Now that you will be looking for defining moments, you will be in a better position to make the most of them. Remember that after we experience one, we are never the same again. But the kind of change we experience will depend on how we respond to those moments. Many of them present us with opportunities. With opportunities come risks, but don't be afraid to take them. It is in moments of risk that the greatest leaders are often born.

≈

I think there is a temptation to believe that all defining moments are highly dramatic and usually occur early in the life of leaders. I don't think that's true. You don't need a lot of major breakthroughs to achieve dramatic results. Just one can make a huge difference. As Albert Einstein used to say, he only came up with the theory of relativity once, but it kept him in pipe tobacco for years.

I believe that if I keep growing, keep seeking opportunities, and keep taking risks, I will continue to experience defining moments. If I keep making good choices and always try to do things that benefit my people in those moments, my leadership will continue to be redefined, to grow, and to improve. When that happens, everybody wins.

———————————— ∾ ————————————

To see a video clip of John Maxwell teaching more on this leadership principle and to access additional helpful tools and information, visit www.johnmaxwell.com/leadershipgold.

Defining Moments Define Your Leadership

APPLICATION EXERCISES

*1. **What is your track record?*** Look back on your life and the decisions you've made at critical moments. What kinds of defining moments have you experienced in the past? Write down as many as you can remember. For each, note:

- The situation
- Your decision or response
- The result

Have your responses been generally good or bad? Is there a common denominator for the poor choices? If you have the courage, ask those closest to you their opinion about your mistakes. If you see a pattern, what is it and how can you address it so that you don't make similar poor choices in the future?

*2. **How are you managing your decisions?*** Using the following list as an example, create a list of choices you will make based on your values and priorities.

Attitude: I will choose and display the right attitudes daily.
Priorities: I will determine and act upon important priorities daily.
Health: I will know and follow healthy guidelines daily.
Family: I will communicate with and care for my family daily.
Thinking: I will practice and develop good thinking daily.
Commitment: I will make and keep proper commitments daily.
Finances: I will earn and properly manage finances daily.
Faith: I will deepen and live out my faith daily.
Relationships: I will initiate and invest in solid relationships daily.

Generosity: I will plan for and model generosity daily.
Values: I will embrace and practice good values daily.
Growth: I will desire and experience improvements daily.

Post your list where you will see it every morning. Review the list daily for a month and manage your moment-to-moment decisions based on your choices.

3. How prepared are you for future defining moments? As you face each day, try to be alert to the kinds of defining moments leaders typically face:

- Ground Breakers—opportunities to do something new
- Heart Breakers—opportunities to reevaluate priorities
- Cloud Breakers—opportunities for a clear vision
- Chart Breakers—opportunities to go to a new level

Think about how you will make the most of these opportunities.

MENTORING MOMENT

The way emerging leaders handle opportunities and crises often defines them. Ask the people you are mentoring to describe how they have handled such moments and to explain how and why they made decisions during those times. Ask how others might define them as a leader based on their actions. If your perception of how it defines them is different from theirs, explain it. If you have observed other defining moments in their leadership that they are unaware of, point them out.

4

---～---

WHEN YOU GET KICKED IN
THE REAR, YOU KNOW
YOU'RE OUT IN FRONT

One of the prices of leadership is criticism. When spectators watch a race, where do they focus their attention? On the front runners! Few people pay close attention to the racers who are out of contention. Racers who are viewed as being out of the running are often ignored or dismissed. But when you're out front and ahead of the crowd, everything you do attracts attention.

As a young leader I wanted to be out front, and I enjoyed the praise of the people. However, I didn't want to put up with anybody's "constructive criticism." Very quickly I learned that I had unrealistic expectations. You don't get one without receiving the other. If you want to be a leader, you need to get used to criticism, because if you are successful, you *will* be criticized. Certain people will always find something to be unhappy about. And the way some people criticize others, you'd think they got paid for it!

Being criticized can be very discouraging. One day when I was feeling down, I shared my weariness of criticism with a friend, and his response was enlightening.

"When you're getting discouraged as a leader," he said, "think of Moses. He led a million complaining people for forty years and never arrived where he was supposed to go." Moses faced a lot of complaints, criticism, and just plain whining. Some days as a leader, I can sympathize with Moses. I bet if he had it to do all over again, he would have made a note to self: next time don't tell Pharaoh to let *all* my people go.

HOW DO YOU HANDLE CRITICISM?

I love the story of the salesman who was getting a haircut and mentioned that he was about to take a trip to Rome, Italy.

"Rome is a terribly overrated city," commented his barber, who was born in northern Italy. "What airline are you taking?"

The salesman told him the name of the airline and the barber responded, "What a terrible airline! Their seats are cramped, their food is bad, and their planes are always late. What hotel are you staying at?"

The salesman named the hotel, and the barber exclaimed, "Why would you stay there? That hotel is in the wrong part of town and has horrible service. You'd be better off staying home!"

"But I expect to close a big deal while I'm there," the salesman replied. "And afterward I hope to see the pope."

"You'll be disappointed trying to do business in Italy," said the barber. "And don't count on seeing the pope. He only grants audiences to very important people."

Three weeks later the salesman returned to the barber shop. "And how was your trip?" asked the barber.

"Wonderful!" replied the salesman. "The flight was perfect, the service at the hotel was excellent, and I made a big sale. And"—the salesman paused for effect—"I got to meet the pope!"

"You got to meet the pope?" Finally, the barber was impressed. "Tell me what happened!"

"Well, when I approached him, I bent down and kissed his ring."

"No kidding! And what did he say?"

"He looked down at my head and said, 'My son, where did you ever get such a lousy haircut?'"

Not everyone handles criticism the same way. Some try to ignore it. Some try to defend themselves against it. Others, like the salesman, use a witty remark to put a critic in his place. But no matter what, if you are a leader, you *will* have to deal with criticism.

How to Hold Up Under Criticism

Since all leaders have to deal with negativity and criticism, regardless of position or profession, it's important for them to learn to handle it constructively. Greek philosopher Aristotle said, "Criticism is something you can avoid easily—by saying nothing, doing nothing, and being nothing." However, that isn't an option for anyone who wants to be successful as a leader. So what do you do? The following four-step process has helped me to deal with criticism, so I pass it on to you.

1. Know Yourself—This Is a Reality Issue

As a young leader I soon learned that having an upfront position was certain to draw criticism, no matter who the leader was or what he did. Highly visible leaders often have to function in difficult environments— such as the office in which the following sign is said to have been displayed:

Notice:
   This department requires no physical fitness program: everyone gets enough exercise jumping to conclusions, flying off the handle, running down the boss, knifing friends in the back, dodging responsibility, and pushing their luck.

—Anonymous

So if you are automatically going to be criticized if you are a leader, what should you do? First, have a realistic view of yourself. That will lay a solid foundation for you to handle criticism successfully. Here's why: Many times, when a leader is being criticized, it's really the leadership position that prompts the negative remarks, not the individual leader. You need to be able to separate the two, and you can do that only when you know yourself. If a criticism is directed at the position, don't take it personally. Let it roll off of you. Knowing yourself well may take some time and effort. As founding father Benjamin Franklin observed, "There are three things extremely hard: steel, a diamond, and to know one's self." However, the effort is worth the reward.

I have to admit that the majority of criticism that I have received over the years was directed more at me than at the position I held. Often people have tried to help me know myself, and the conversation usually began with the phrase "I'm going to tell you something for your own good." I discovered that when they tell me something for my own good, they never seem to have anything good to tell me! However, I have also realized that what I need to hear most is what I want to hear least. From those conversations I have learned much about myself, including the following:

> *"Criticism is something you can avoid easily— by saying nothing, doing nothing, and being nothing."*
> —*Aristotle*

- I am impatient.
- I am unrealistic about the time tasks take and how difficult most processes are.
- I don't like to give a lot of time or effort to people's emotional concerns.
- I overestimate the ability of others.
- I assume too much.
- I want to delegate responsibility too quickly.
- I want options—so many that I drive everyone crazy.
- I don't care for rules or restrictions.
- I determine my priorities quickly and expect others to have similar attitudes.
- I process issues quickly and want to move on—even when other people aren't ready to.

Obviously, the things I have found out about myself are not flattering. Yet those weaknesses are a reality. So the question is, what am I to do about it?

2. Change Yourself—This Is a Responsibility Issue

When someone's criticism about me is accurate, then I have a responsibility to do something about it. That is part of being a good leader. If I respond correctly to my critics by examining myself and admitting my short-comings, then I set myself up to begin making positive changes in my life.

Author Aldous Huxley remarked, "You shall know the truth and the truth shall make you mad." My first natural reaction to criticism often isn't good—it's sometimes hurt, but more often anger. But after my anger has subsided, I try to determine whether the criticism is constructive or destructive. (Some say constructive criticism is when I criticize you, but destructive criticism is when you criticize me!) Here are the questions I ask to determine what kind of criticism it is:

- *Who criticized me?* Adverse criticism from a wise person is more to be desired than the enthusiastic approval of a fool. The source often matters.
- *How was the criticism given?* I try to discern whether the person was being judgmental or whether he gave me the benefit of the doubt and spoke with kindness.
- *Why was it given?* Was it given out of a personal hurt or for my benefit? Hurting people hurt people; they lash out or criticize to try to make themselves feel better, not to help the other person.

Whether the criticism is legitimate or not, what determines whether I grow from or groan under unwanted words is my attitude. My friend, management expert Ken Blanchard, is right when he says, "Some leaders are like seagulls. When something goes wrong, they fly in, make a lot of noise, and crap all over everything." People with that kind of attitude not only refuse to take responsibility for their contribution to the problem, but they also make conditions terrible for the people who work with them.

People can change for the better only when they are open to improvement. For that reason, when I am criticized I try to maintain the right attitude by

- not being defensive,
- looking for the grain of truth,
- making the necessary changes, and
- taking the high road.

If I do those things, there is a very good chance that I will learn things about myself, improve as a leader, and preserve the relationships I have with others.

3. Accept Yourself—This Is a Maturity Issue

Jonas Salk, developer of the Salk polio vaccine, had many critics in spite of his incredible contribution to medicine. Of criticism, he observed, "First people will tell you that you are wrong. Then they will tell you that you are right, but what you're doing really isn't important. Finally, they will admit that you are right and that what you are doing is very important; but after all, they knew it all the time." How do leaders who are out front handle this kind of fickle response from others? They learn to accept themselves. If you have endeavored to know yourself, and have worked hard to change yourself, then what more can you do?

> *"You shall know the truth and the truth shall make you mad."*
> *—Aldous Huxley*

Professor and author Leo Buscaglia counseled, "The easiest thing to be in the world is you. The most difficult thing to be is what other people want you to be. Don't let them put you in that position." To be the best person you can be—and the best leader—you need to be yourself. That doesn't mean that you aren't willing to grow and change. It just means that you work to become the best *you* that you can be. And as psychologist Carl Rogers remarked, "The curious paradox is that when I accept myself just as I am, then I can change." Being who you really are is the first step in becoming better than you are.

Because I've already written about working within your strength zone, which you can do only if you know and accept who you are, I don't need to say a lot more about it here, other than to emphasize that accepting yourself is a sign of maturity. If you worry about what other people think of you, it's because you have more confidence in their opinion than you have in your own. Executive coach and consultant Judith Bardwick says, "Real confidence comes from knowing and accepting yourself—your strengths and limitations—in contrast to depending on affirmation from others."

4. Forget Yourself—This Is a Security Issue

The final step in the process of effectively handling criticism is to stop focusing on yourself. When we were growing up, a lot of us spent a good deal of time worrying about what the world thought of us. Now I'm sixty, and I realize the world really wasn't paying much attention.

Secure people forget about themselves so they can focus on others. By doing this, they can face nearly any kind of criticism—and even serve the critic. For years when I was the pastor of churches, I went out of my way to initiate personal contact with my critics every Sunday. I sought them out and greeted them. I wanted them to know that I valued them as people, regardless of what their attitude was toward me. Being secure in who I am and focusing on others allows me to take the high road with people. I try to live out a sentiment expressed by Parkenham Beatty, who advised, "By your own soul learn to live. And if men thwart you, take no heed. If men hate you, have no care: Sing your song, dream your dream, hope your hope and pray your prayer."

Being who you really are is the first step in becoming better than you are.

One day Perry Noble, a young leader whom I have the privilege of mentoring, shared with me about the hurt he felt when others criticized him. I could identify with his feelings. When he asked for advice about how to respond to criticism, I explained that a secure leader never needs to defend himself.

Perry later said to me, "That day I realized I was spending way too much time defending myself to my critics and not getting done what I really needed to get done." Once again, I could relate.

As leaders, we must always be serious about our responsibilities, but it isn't healthy for us to take ourselves too seriously. A Chinese proverb says, "Blessed are those who can laugh at themselves. They shall never cease to be entertained." I must say, for years I have entertained myself.

My friend Joyce Meyer observes, "God will help you be all you can be, but He will never let you be successful at becoming someone else." We can't do more than try to be all that we can be. If we do that as leaders, we will give others our best, and we will sometimes take hits from others. But that's okay. That is the price for being out front.

APPLICATION EXERCISES

1. What are your deficiencies? Where do you fall short as a person and leader? If you can't answer that question, then you don't really know yourself. And if you don't, how will you be able to accept what you cannot change or change what you must to be a better leader? Ask five trustworthy people who know you where you come up short. Then decide what you need to change and what you need to accept.

2. How secure are you as a leader? Insecurity and defensiveness are two characteristics that I have seen prevent many leaders from reaching their potential. When others criticize you, is your first reaction to dismiss what's said, defend yourself, or fight back? If so, your responses may hold you back as a leader. Practice quietness the next time you are criticized. Take in all that's said, tell the person that you will think about the criticism, and then take some time to process it on your own.

3. How can you properly process criticism? Use the three questions from the chapter to determine whether some criticism can be helpful to you:

- Who criticized me?
- How was the criticism given?
- Why was it given?

As you ask these questions, start out by giving the critic the benefit of the doubt so that you can be as objective as possible. If the criticism is well founded, then consider how you can make changes to improve.

MENTORING MOMENT

Observe how the people you are mentoring handle criticism—not just from you or others who are above them in the leadership hierarchy, but also from those who work with them and for them. How do they respond? Are they open to improvement and change when it's not their own idea? Are they gracious when receiving negative feedback? Do they put the team ahead of their own egos? When they know that the vision is right, do they treat their critics graciously and take the high road with them? Share your observations with them and give them concrete suggestions for improvement.

5

NEVER WORK A DAY
IN YOUR LIFE

People often ask me the key to my success. Setting aside for the moment the whole question of what it means to be successful, my answer is usually quite simple. I love what I do! We have all heard the advice: find something you like to do so much that you would gladly do it for nothing; then learn to do it so well that people are happy to pay you for it. That's what I've done in my career. I feel like Thomas Edison, who said, "I never did a day's work in my life. It was all fun!"

FOLLOWING MY PASSION

Following your passion is the key to finding your potential. You will not achieve the latter without pursuing the former. I remember well the incident that caused me to make the connection between passion and potential in my own life. It occurred in Hillham, Indiana, where I took my first job. I was the pastor of a small country church there. It wasn't much to look at. The church building was more than a hundred years old. The roof sagged and the walls bowed. The first Sunday I was there three people attended the service—and two of them were my wife, Margaret, and me! Most leaders would have been discouraged with the situation, but not me.

My passion to grow a congregation in that farming community knew no bounds. When friends came to visit Margaret and me, I immediately took them over to our church for a tour, which took all of about thirty seconds! I wasn't worried about the location, the old building, the small attendance, or even my lack of experience. I was filled with passion. I wanted to help people.

Following your passion is the key to finding your potential.

Over the next several months, my passion spread to the community. The church began to fill up on Sundays. Momentum was increasing, and I could sense that it was time to really stretch the congregation. So I challenged them to set an attendance goal of 300 people on the first Sunday in October. Though all the members were willing to help, most of them felt that the goal was unreachable. Our small building seated only 100 people, our tiny parking lot held only thirty-three cars, and the highest attendance in the church's history had been 135 people.

In spite of the odds, everyone gave it their best. We invited everyone we knew. When the day finally arrived, excitement mounted as people kept coming onto the property. Many could not even get into the building. Right before I was scheduled to speak, the lay leader announced the attendance: "Today we have 299 people."

The people cheered. It was beyond their greatest expectations, far exceeding anything they had ever done before. But I was not satisfied. With perhaps more passion than wisdom, I stood up and asked, "What was our goal for today?"

"Three hundred," the crowd responded.

"Well, if 300 was our goal," I declared, "then 300 is how many we will have. You sing a few more songs, and I will go out and find one more person. *Then* we will finish the service."

As I strode down the aisle toward the door, the people cheered wildly and patted me on the back. I was pumped. It felt like I was going through the team's tunnel out into the stadium for the Super Bowl—until I found myself outside. My enthusiasm had taken me into new territory.

"Now what am I going to do?" I asked myself. I was faced with the reality of the task before me.

I looked and saw two men sitting in front of the service station across the street: Sandy Burton, the owner, and Glenn Harris, who worked for him. I walked over to them.

"Did you reach your goal?" Sandy asked before I even finished crossing the road. Everyone in the county knew about it.

"Not yet," I replied. "We have 299 people over there," I said pointing back toward the church. "I need one more person to attend the church for us to meet our goal. Which one of you would like to be the hero for this entire valley?"

They looked at each other and Sandy said, "We both would!"

Sandy put a "closed" sign on the door of his service station, and the three of us walked over to the church. When we entered the building, the place exploded. What everyone wanted but no one expected had actually come to pass.

CREATING A BREAKTHROUGH

The people in that small town in southern Indiana changed that day. And so did I. We had accomplished the impossible. That evening as I reflected on the day, I realized that passion was what took us to the next level. The power of passion had made the difference. It took a significant event and turned it into an unforgettable one. It caused me to take action in a way that I would not have ordinarily done. It motivated two men who never attended church to attend. It created a win for a group of people that improved their self-image and boosted their confidence. It was a day in which all of us became aware that our potential was much greater than we had thought.

> *"Don't put live eggs under dead chickens."*
> *—Howard Hendricks*

When a person doesn't have passion, life can become pretty monotonous. Everything is a "have to" and nothing is a "want to." We feel like little Eddie whose grandmother loved opera and had season tickets every year. When Eddie turned eight, his grandmother decided it was time to take him with her, so she did for his birthday present. She beamed as Eddie squirmed through the entire performance of a somber German opera—sung in German!

The next day, Eddie's mother told him to write a thank-you note to his grandmother. Here is what it said:

> Dear Grandmother,
>   Thank you for the birthday present. It is what I always wanted, but not very much.
>   Love,
>   Eddie

Passion is an incredible asset for any person, but especially for leaders. It keeps us going when others quit. It becomes contagious and influences others to follow us. It pushes us through the toughest of times and gives us energy we did not know we possessed. It fuels us in ways that the following assets can't:

Talent . . . is never enough to enable us to reach our potential. There are many people in the world with great natural talent who never achieve personal or professional success. I feel so strongly about this that I wrote an entire book about it called *Talent Is Never Enough.* To be a successful leader—to be a successful person—you need more than just talent.

Opportunity . . . will never get us to the top by itself. Opportunities may open the door, but the success journey is often long and difficult. Without the passion that sustains when times get tough, people don't make the most of their opportunities and they never reach their potential. As my friend Howard Hendricks says, "Don't put live eggs under dead chickens." That's what opportunities are to people without passion.

Knowledge . . . can be a great asset, but it won't make us "all we can be." Being smart doesn't make someone a leader. Neither does possessing credentials or college degrees. Some of America's worst presidents are reputed to have been the smartest. Some of the greatest, such as Abraham Lincoln, had very little formal education. Formal education doesn't make you a leader. I possess three college degrees including a doctorate, but I believe they have contributed very little to my success as a leader.

A great team . . . can fall short. It's true that leaders cannot be successful without a good team. But having a good team does not guarantee success. A team with no heart and fuzzy leadership won't succeed. Besides, if a team starts out strong but has a weak, passionless leader, the team will eventually become weak and passionless. As the Law of Magnetism says in *The 21 Irrefutable Laws of Leadership*, "We attract who we are, not who we want."

What does a leader need to succeed? Passion. Passion is a real difference-maker. It separates the extraordinary from the ordinary. When I think back on my career, I recognize that passion has enabled me to do the following:

- Believe things I would not have believed
- Feel things I would not have felt
- Attempt things I would not have attempted
- Accomplish things I would not have accomplished
- Meet people I would not have met
- Motivate people I would not have motivated
- Lead people I would not have led

Passion has made an incredible difference in my life. As former GE CEO Jack Welch says, "The world will belong to passionate, driven leaders . . . people who not only have enormous amounts of energy, but who can energize those whom they lead." In all my years of observing people, I have yet to meet an individual who reached his potential but didn't possess passion.

FORGET THE MONEY—FOLLOW YOUR PASSION

In his book *Making a Life, Making a Living*, Mark Albion writes about a revealing study of businesspeople who took two very different paths after graduating from college. Here is what he says:

A study of business school graduates tracked the careers of 1,500 people from 1960 to1980. From the beginning, the graduates were grouped into two categories. Category A consisted of people who said they wanted to make money first so that they could do what they really wanted to do later—after they had taken care of their financial concerns. Those in

Category B pursued their true interests first, sure that the money would eventually follow.

What percentage fell into each category?

Of the 1,500 graduates in the survey, the money-now Category A's comprised 83 percent, or 1,245 people. Category B risk takers made up 17 percent, or 255 graduates.

After twenty years there were 101 millionaires in the group. One came from Category A, 100 from Category B.

The study's author, Srully Blotnick, concluded that "the overwhelming majority of people who have become wealthy have become so thanks to work they found profoundly absorbing. . . . Their 'luck' arose from the accidental dedication they had to an area they enjoyed."[1]

When people pursue what they are truly passionate about, it makes all the difference. Passion fills them with energy and desire. It gives them the will to win. And as writer David Ambrose says, "If you have the will to win, you have achieved half of your success. If you don't, you have achieved half of your failure." If you want to reach your potential, find your passion.

> *"The world will belong to passionate, driven leaders . . . people who not only have enormous amounts of energy, but who can energize those whom they lead."*
> —*Jack Welch*

I believe I have been fortunate because my passion has been my calling and career. Way back at Hillham, I discovered the connection between passion and potential. For almost forty years I have lived off of the energy that comes from loving what I do and doing what I love.

To most people, there's a big difference between work and play. Work is what they *have* to do to earn a living so that someday they can do what they *want* to do. Don't live your life that way! Choose to do what you love and make the necessary adjustments to make it work in your life. Follow the advice of Confucius, who said, "Choose work you love, and you will never have to work a day in your life." The greatest job is one where you're not sure where the line is between work and play.

APPLICATION EXERCISES

1. What is your true passion? What do you love doing so much that you would do it for free? If you've never thought about it before, brainstorm a list.

2. How much passion do you have for your current work? Does your job feel more like work or play? Every job has its negative characteristics, and no job is fun *all* of the time. But the right job should not feel like a chore all the time. What percentage of the time would you consider your job to be enjoyable? Use the following scale to judge the fit of what you're currently doing:

90% or above: You are in your sweet spot—celebrate!
75%–89%: Make minor adjustments to align with your passion.
50%–74%: You need to make major adjustments.
49% or less: You need a job or career change.

3. How can you follow your passion? If you are not in the 90 percent-plus category, you need to try to assess what kinds of adjustments to make. Sometimes taking a different job within the same organization sets a person on the right track. Other times an organization change helps. If you are in the 50 percent or less category, consider trying to transition from your current career track to the activity you thought about when answering the first application question above.

No matter which category you fall into, think through and write out in detail the steps that would be required for you to make a transition.

Mentoring Moment

Most people in the workplace are used to working for bosses who care only about the work they get done, not about them as human beings. Most have never had a leader who desired to help them find their passion and unique purpose in life. You can be the one to change that. Sit down and talk to the people you are mentoring, asking them questions about what's most important to them. Share your own observations with them as well. Be open to the possibility of helping them transition to another position, department, or organization if there isn't a good fit where they are currently.

6

THE BEST LEADERS
ARE LISTENERS

Steven Sample, in his book *The Contrarian's Guide to Leadership*, writes, "The average person suffers from three delusions: (1) that he is a good driver, (2) that he has a good sense of humor, and (3) that he is a good listener." I plead guilty on all three counts!

I will never forget the time a lady I worked with confronted me about my poor listening skills. She said, "John, when people talk to you, often you seem distracted and look around the room. We're not sure that you are listening to us!"

I was surprised because, like most people, I *really did* think I was a good listener. The first thing I did was apologize. I trusted the opinion of the person who had confronted me, and I knew it had taken courage for her to tell me. (I was her boss.) The second thing I did was start trying to change. For several years I made it a regular practice to put an "L" in the corner of my legal pad anytime I was in a meeting to remind myself to *listen*. Sometimes I would write "LL" to remind myself to *look* at them while I listened. It made a big difference in my leadership.

Steven Sample says, "Many leaders are terrible listeners; they actually think talking is more important than listening. But contrarian leaders know it is better to listen first and talk later. And when they listen, they do so artfully."

The positive benefits of being a good listener are much more valuable than we often recognize. Recently I read a humorous story that Jim Lange included in his book *Bleedership*.

A couple of rednecks are out in the woods hunting when one of them falls to the ground. He doesn't seem to be breathing and his eyes are rolled back in his head.

The other guy whips out his cell phone and calls 911.

He frantically tells the operator, "Bubba is dead! What can I do?"

The operator, in a calm, soothing voice says, "Just take it easy. I can help. First, let's make sure he's dead."

There is silence, and then a shot is heard.

The guy's voice comes back on the line and says, "Okay, now what?"

As this story about rednecks illustrates—we can hear what is said without really listening to what is being communicated. The hunter above heard what the operator told him and technically did make sure that his hunting companion was dead. But had he really been listening, I don't think he would have shot his partner.[1]

The story may seem silly, but it contains an important truth. When we hear without really listening, our leadership is bound to suffer—and so will our followers.

I once read about a study that stated that we hear half of what is being said, listen to half of what we hear, understand half of it, believe half of that, and remember only half of that. If you translate those assumptions into an eight-hour work day, here is what it would mean:

- You spend half your day—about four hours—in listening activities.
- You hear about two hours' worth of what is said.
- You actually listen to an hour of it.
- You understand only thirty minutes of that hour.
- You believe only fifteen minutes' worth.
- And you remember less than eight minutes of all that is said.

That's a pretty poor track record. And it shows that we all need to work much harder at actively listening!

WHY LISTENERS ARE MORE EFFECTIVE LEADERS

Because of my desire to be a more effective listener, I have actively observed leaders for years and paid close attention to how the effective ones listen to others. And I have come to some conclusions about the impact of good listening related to leadership.

1. Understanding People Precedes Leading Them

Leadership finds its source in understanding. To be worthy of the responsibility of leadership, a person must have insight into the human heart. Sensitivity toward the hopes and dreams of people on your team is essential for connecting with them and motivating them. In my book *The 21 Irrefutable Laws of Leadership*, I write about the Law of Connection, which states, "Leaders touch a heart before they ask for a hand." You cannot connect with someone if you don't try to listen to and understand them. Not only is it not fair to ask for the help of someone with whom you haven't connected, it is also ineffective. If you want to be more effective connecting with people, make it your goal to understand them.

> *Leadership finds its source in understanding.*

2. Listening Is the Best Way to Learn

It is no accident that we have one mouth and two ears. When we fail to listen, we shut off much of our learning potential. You've probably heard the phrase "seeing is believing." Well, so is listening. Talk show host Larry King said, "I remind myself every morning: nothing I say this day will teach me anything. So, if I'm going to learn, I must do it by listening."

In 1997 we moved to Atlanta, Georgia. Immediately I realized the influence of the African American community upon that city. I wanted to connect with people in that community and learn about their journey. I asked my friend Sam Chand to set up four lunches with some top African American leaders. For me, it was one of the greatest learning experiences of my life.

Our time together was filled with our getting acquainted, my asking questions, and my listening to wonderful stories. I left each lunch with new friends and greater respect for the people I met and for their life experiences. Many individuals expressed their surprise to me that with my leadership experience, I did not try to teach them about leadership, but that I was the student and they were the teachers. If I had done that, I wouldn't have learned anything. Today I am still listening to and learning from many of the leaders who became my friends at those lunches.

3. Listening Can Keep Problems from Escalating

A Cherokee proverb says, "Listen to the whispers and you won't have to hear the screams." Good leaders are attentive to small issues. They pay attention to their intuition. And they also pay close attention to what *isn't* being said. That requires more than just good listening skills. It requires a good understanding of people, and it also means being secure enough to ask for honest communication from others and to not become defensive when receiving it. To be an effective leader, you need to let others tell you what you *need* to hear, not necessarily what you *want* to hear.

Gordon Bethune, former CEO of Continental Airlines, took this idea a step further when he advised, "Make sure you only hire people who will be willing to kick the door open if you lose direction and close it. You may be able to ignore somebody's opinion if you don't like it, but if the person has the data to back it up, your intellect should be able to overwhelm your vanity."[2]

> *"Listen to the whispers and you won't have to hear the screams."*
> —*Cherokee proverb*

A common fault that occurs in people as they gain more authority is impatience with those who work for them. Leaders like results. Unfortunately, that action orientation sometimes causes them to stop listening. But a deaf ear is the first symptom of a closed mind, and having a closed mind is a surefire way to hurt your leadership.

The higher people go in leadership, the more authority they wield, and the less they are *forced* to listen to others. However, their *need* to listen becomes greater than ever! The farther leaders get from the front lines, the more they must depend on others for accurate information. If they haven't formed the habit of listening—carefully and intelligently—they aren't going to get the facts they need. And when a leader stays in the dark, whatever problems the organization is having will only get worse.

4. Listening Establishes Trust

Effective leaders are always good communicators, but that means much more than just being a good talker. David Burns, a medical doctor and professor of psychiatry at the University of Pennsylvania, points out, "The biggest mistake you can make in trying to talk convincingly is to put your highest priority on expressing your ideas and feelings. What most people really want is to be listened to, respected, and understood. The moment people see that they are being understood, they become more motivated to understand your point of view."

Author and speaker Brian Tracy says, "Listening builds trust, the foundation of all lasting relationships." When my employee confronted me about my poor listening skills, what she was really telling me was that I was not trustworthy. She didn't know whether her ideas, opinions, and feelings were safe with me. By becoming a more attentive listener, I was able to earn her trust.

> *"Listening builds trust, the foundation of all lasting relationships."*
> *—Brian Tracy*

When leaders listen to followers and use what they hear to make improvements that benefit those who speak up and the organization, then followers put their trust in those leaders. When leaders do the opposite—when they fail to listen—it damages the leader-follower relationship. When followers no longer believe that their leaders are listening to them, they start looking for someone who will.

5. Listening Can Improve the Organization

The bottom line is that when the leader listens, the organization gets better. Former Chrysler chairman Lee Iacocca asserted, "Listening can make the difference between a mediocre company and a great one." That means listening to people up and down the line at every level of the organization—to customers, workers, and other leaders.

Dallas-based Chili's, one of the nation's top restaurant chains, has prided itself in having leaders who listen. Norman Brinker, onetime owner and chairman of Chili's, believes that responsive communication is the key to good relations with both employees and customers. He also has learned that such communication pays big dividends. Almost 80 percent of Chili's menu has come from suggestions made by unit managers.

Listening always pays dividends. The more you know, the better off you are—as long as you maintain perspective and think like a leader. Niccolo Machiavelli, author of *The Prince*, wrote, "Minds are of three kinds. One is capable of thinking for itself; another is able to understand the thinking of others; and a third can neither think for itself nor understand the thinking of others. The first is of the highest excellence, the second is excellent, and the third is worthless." To be a good leader, you must be able to not only think for yourself but also understand and learn from the thinking of others.

Is it possible to be a leader without being a listener? The answer is yes. Talk to employees in companies all across the country, and they will tell you that they work for people who do not listen to them. Is it possible to be a *good* leader without listening? The answer is no. No one can go to the highest level and take his or her organization there without being a good listener. It simply doesn't happen, because you can never get the best out of people if you don't know who they are, where they want to go, why they care, how they think, and what they have to contribute. You can learn those things only if you listen.

Author and speaker Jim Rohn says, "One of the greatest gifts you can give anyone is the gift of attention." I believe that's true. But listening to followers isn't just a gift to them. It benefits the leader too. When leaders listen, they receive others' insight, knowledge, wisdom, and respect. That puts all of an organization's assets into play, ready to be marshaled for the fulfillment of the vision and the attainment of its goals. What a wonderful gift.

To see a video clip of John Maxwell teaching more on this leadership principle and to access additional helpful tools and information, visit www.johnmaxwell.com/leadershipgold.

APPLICATION EXERCISES

1. Give yourself a listening audit. The next few times you are in meetings, ask your assistant or a colleague to track how many minutes you spend speaking and how many minutes you spend listening. If you're not spending at least 80 percent of the time listening, you need to improve. Try writing "L" on your notes where you will see it.

2. Who doesn't feel listened to? If people you work or live with feel that you do not listen to them, you will be able to see it in their faces. Think about the people who are most important to you in your life. The next time you have a conversation with them, stop everything you're doing, give them your undivided attention, and look them in the eye as they speak. If you see surprise, avoidance, or hostility in their expression, it may be because they feel you have not really listened to them in the past. Start a dialogue on the subject. Ask if you've neglected to listen in the past, and then let them talk. Don't defend yourself. Seek only clarification and apologize if necessary.

3. What people have you neglected to seek out? Effective leaders are *active* listeners. By that I mean that they do more than listen to people who approach them with something to say. They seek out the thoughts, opinions, and feelings of others—starting with the top leaders who work for and with them. If you haven't heard from some of your key people recently, seek them out and give them your ear.

MENTORING MOMENT

Give each of the people you are mentoring a listening assignment. Ask them to take on the role of "focused listener" at a meeting you are both attending. Tell them their assignment is to (1) take written notes of what is discussed at the meeting; (2) look for and record nonverbal cues and feedback of meeting participants; and (3) take note of anything they sense in the room and of what *isn't* being said. After the meeting, ask for their insights and conclusions. Then share with them all the dynamics you observed.

7

GET IN THE ZONE
AND STAY THERE

Can you remember the first lesson you ever learned about leadership? I can. It came from my dad. He used to tell my brother, my sister, and me, "Find out what you do well and keep on doing it." That wasn't just casual advice. He and my mother made it their mission to help us discover our strengths and start developing them before we were old enough to leave home and go out on our own.

Dad also reinforced that advice by living it. One of his favorite sayings was "This one thing I do." He had an uncanny ability to remain focused within his areas of strength. That, coupled with his determination to finish what he started, served him well throughout his career and beyond. He stays in his strength zone. It is one of the reasons he has always been the greatest inspiration for my life.

SEARCHING FOR STRENGTHS

When I started my career, I was committed to finding my strength zone and working to stay in it. However, I was frustrated for my first few years working. Like many inexperienced leaders, I tried to do many different things to discover what I really could do well. In addition, people's expectations for what I would do and how I would lead did not always match my strengths. My responsibilities and obligations sometimes required that I perform tasks for which I possessed neither talent nor skill. I was often ineffective as a result. It took me several years to sort all this out, find my strength zone, and recruit and develop other people to compensate for my weaknesses.

If you are a young leader and you are still uncertain about where your strengths lie, don't get discouraged. Be patient and keep working it out. Here's what I know: no matter if you're just starting out or if you are at the peak of your career, the more you work in your strength zone, the more successful you will be.

Defining Personal Success

I've heard many definitions of success from many people over the years. In fact, I've embraced different definitions myself at different stages of my life. But in the last fifteen years, I have zeroed in on a definition that I think captures success no matter who people are or what they want to do. I believe success is

Knowing your purpose in life,
Growing to your maximum potential, and
Sowing seeds that benefit others.

If you are able to do those three things, you are successful. However, none of them is possible unless you find and stay in your strength zone.

I love the story of a group of neighborhood boys who built a tree house and formed their own club. When the grown-ups were told who had been selected for which office, they were astonished to hear that a four-year-old had been elected president.

"That boy must be a born leader," one dad observed. "How did it happen that all you bigger boys voted for him?"

"Well, you see, Dad," his son replied, "he can't very well be secretary because he doesn't know how to read or write. He couldn't be treasurer, because he can't count. He would never do for sergeant at arms because he's too little to throw anybody out. If we didn't choose him for anything, he'd feel bad. So we made him president."

Real life, of course, doesn't work that way. You don't become an effective leader by default. You must be intentional. And you must work from your strengths.

Whenever I mentor people and help them discover their purpose, I always encourage them to start the process by discovering their strengths, not exploring their shortcomings. Why? Because people's purpose in life is always connected to their giftedness. It always works that way. You are not called to do something that you have no talent for. You will discover your purpose by finding and remaining in your strength zone.

> *People's purpose in life is always connected to their giftedness.*

Similarly, you cannot grow to your maximum potential if you continually work outside of your strength zone. Improvement is always related to ability. The greater your natural ability, the greater your potential for improvement. I've known people who thought that reaching their potential would come from shoring up their weaknesses. But do you know what happens when you spend all your time working on your weaknesses and never developing your strengths? If you work really hard, you might claw your way all the way up to mediocrity! But you'll never get beyond it. Nobody admires or rewards mediocrity.

The final piece of the puzzle—living a life that benefits others—always depends upon us giving our best, not our worst. You can't change the world by giving only leftovers or by performing with mediocrity. Only your best will add value to others and lift them up.

FINDING YOUR OWN STRENGTH ZONE

British poet and lexicographer Samuel Johnson said, "Almost every man wastes part of his life in attempts to display qualities which he does not possess." If you have an image in your mind of what talents people are supposed to have, yet you do not possess them, then you will have a difficult time finding your true strengths. You need to discover and develop who *you* are. Here are a few suggestions to help you:

1. Ask, "What Am I Doing Well?"

People who reach their potential spend less time asking, "What am I doing right?" and more time asking, "What am I doing well?" The first is a moral question; the second is a talent question. You should always strive to do what's right. But doing what's right doesn't tell you anything about your talent.

2. Get Specific

When we consider our strengths, we tend to think too broadly. Peter Drucker, the father of modern management, writes, "The great mystery isn't that people do things badly but that they occasionally do a few things well. The only thing that is universal is incompetence. Strength is always specific! Nobody ever commented, for example, that the great violinist Jascha Heifetz probably couldn't play the trumpet well." The more specific you can get about your strengths, the better the chance you can find your "sweet spot." Why be on the fringes of your strength zone when you have a chance to be right in the center?

3. Listen for What Others Praise

Many times we take our talents for granted. We think because we can do something well, anyone can. Often that's not true. How can you tell when you're overlooking a skill or talent? Listen to what others say. Your strengths will capture the attention of others and draw them to you. On the other hand, when you're working in areas of weakness, few people will show interest. If others are continually praising you in a particular area, start developing it.

4. Check Out the Competition

You don't want to spend all your time comparing yourself to others; that's not healthy. But you don't want to waste your time doing something that others do much better. Former GE CEO Jack Welch asserts, "If you don't have a competitive advantage, don't compete." People don't pay for average. If you don't have the talent to do something better than the competition, place your focus elsewhere.

To get a better picture of where you stand in relationship to the competition, ask yourself the following questions:

- Are others doing what I am doing?
- Are they doing it well?

• Are they doing it better than I am?
• Can I become better than they are?
• If I do become better, what will be the result?
• If I don't become better, what will be the result?

The answer to the last question is: you lose. Why? Because your competition is working in their strength zone and you aren't!

Former all-star baseball catcher Jim Sundberg advised, "Discover your uniqueness, then discipline yourself to develop it." That's what I've tried to do. Many years ago I realized that one of my strengths was communicating. People have always been motivated when they hear me speak. After a while, many opportunities were given to me to speak at events with other motivational speakers. At first it was very intimidating because they were so good. But as I listened to them, the thing I kept asking myself was, "What can I do that will set me apart from them?" I felt it might not be possible for me to be better than they were, but it would be possible for me to be different. Over time I discovered and developed that difference. I would strive to be a motivational *teacher*, not just a motivation *speaker*. I wanted

> *"Discover your uniqueness, then discipline yourself to develop it."*
> *—Jim Sundberg*

people not only to enjoy what I shared but to also be able to apply what I taught to their lives. For more than two decades, I have disciplined my life to develop that uniqueness. It's my niche—my strength zone.

TO BE A SUCCESSFUL LEADER, FIND AND DEVELOP THE STRENGTH ZONES OF YOUR PEOPLE

Whenever you see people who are successful in their work, you can rest assured that they are working in their strength zone. But that's not enough if you want to be successful as a leader. Good leaders help others find their strength zones and empower them to work in them. In fact, the best leaders are characterized by the ability to recognize the special abilities and limitations of others, and the capacity to fit their people into the jobs where they will do best.

Sadly, most people are not working in their areas of strength and therefore are not reaching their potential. The Gallup organization conducted research on 1.7 million people in the workplace. According to their findings, only 20 percent of employees feel that their strengths are in play every day in the work setting.[1] In my opinion, that is largely the fault of their leaders. They have failed to help their people find their strengths and place them in the organization where their strengths can be an asset to the company.

> *"Organizations exist to make people's strengths effective and their weaknesses irrelevant. And this is the work of effective leaders."*
> —Frances Hesselbein

In her book *Hesselbein on Leadership*, Frances Hesselbein, the chairman of the board of governors of the Leader to Leader Institute founded by Peter F. Drucker, writes, "Peter Drucker reminds us that organizations exist to make people's strengths effective and their weaknesses irrelevant. And this is the work of effective leaders. Drucker also tells us that there may be born leaders but there are far too few to depend on them."

If you desire to be an effective leader, you must develop the ability to develop people in their areas of strength. How do you do that?

Study and know the people on your team.

What are your people's strengths and weaknesses? Whom do they relate to on the team? Are they growing and do they have more growth potential in the area in which they're working? Is their attitude an asset or a liability? Do they love what they do and are they doing it well? These are questions that must be answered by the leader.

Communicate to individuals how they fit on the team.

What are the strengths that they bring to the table? Are there times their contribution will be especially valuable? How do they complement the other members of the team? What do they need from the other players that will complement their weaknesses? The more that people know how they fit on a team, the more they will desire to properly make the most of their fit and maximize their contribution.

Communicate to all team members how each player fits on the team.

It's obvious that you can't have a winning team without teamwork. However, not every leader takes steps to help team members work together. If you communicate to all the players how all the people fit together and what strengths they bring for their role, then teammates will value and respect one another.

Emphasize completing one another above competing with one another.

Healthy competition between teammates is good. It presses them to do their best. But in the end, team members need to work together for the sake of the team, not only for themselves.

To some leaders, the idea of focusing almost entirely on strengths seems counterintuitive. Several years ago I was spending a day with leaders of several companies, and one of the subjects I addressed was the importance of staying in your strength zone. I repeatedly encouraged them not to work with their areas of weakness related to ability. During the Q&A session, a CEO pushed back against the idea. The example he used was that of Tiger Woods.

"When Tiger plays a bad round of golf," he observed, "he goes straight to the driving range and practices for hours. You see, John, he's working on his weaknesses."

"No," I replied, "he's working on his strengths. Tiger is the greatest golfer in the world. He's practicing golf shots. He's not practicing accounting or music or basketball. He is working on a weakness within his strength zone. That will always produce positive results."

Working on a weakness in your strength zone will always produce greater results than working on a strength in a weak area. I love golf, but if I practice golf shots, I will never greatly improve. Why? Because I'm an average golfer. Practice won't make perfect—it will make permanent! If I want to make progress, I need to keep working on my leadership and communication. Those are my strength zones.

Where are yours? If you're spending time in them, then you are making an investment into your success.

APPLICATION EXERCISES

1. Have you identified your strength zone? If you and I were able to sit down and talk, would you be able to tell me your strengths? How specific would you be able to be? The older and more experienced you are, the more specific you should be able to be. If you are not sure of your strengths, follow the suggestions in the chapter: think about what you are doing well, listen to what colleagues say about your talents, and analyze where you have an edge over your competition.

2. Is your job utilizing your strengths? List three things you do well in your job. Now ask yourself these three questions:

- Are you doing them more or less?
- Are you developing them more or less?
- Are you bringing others around who complement your strengths?

If you answer no to any of those questions, you need to become more intentional about getting into your strength zone.

3. Are you leading team members into their strength zones? If you are a leader, your team is depending on you to help them find and stay in their strength zones. What have you done with each person to facilitate this? If you can't cite specific actions, then you need to immediately follow the suggestions in the chapter to help them.

MENTORING MOMENT

Sit down with each person you're mentoring to discuss their strengths. Ask them to describe them. Give them feedback based on their past performance and your observations. Help to dispel any misconceptions they have about themselves. And assign them responsibilities that will make the most of their strengths. If your people have already identified their strengths and are already working in them, then help them create a strategy to identify, encourage, and develop the strengths of *their* people and hold them accountable for following through on it.

8

A LEADER'S FIRST
RESPONSIBILITY IS TO
DEFINE REALITY

The first time I heard that it is the leader's responsibility to define reality was from leadership expert and author Max DePree. His assertion made sense to me instantly, and I agreed with it. But that doesn't mean I was naturally good at it.

Of all the lessons I've learned about leadership, this one has been the most difficult. I could be the poster child for positive thinking. I am wired to give hope and encourage others. I just can't help myself. As a result, my philosophy has been a little like that of humorist Garrison Keillor, who said, "Sometimes you have to look reality in the eye and deny it." Truthfully, my aversion to being realistic and my occasional reluctance to embrace the fact that it is a leader's responsibility to define reality has cost me greatly. But at the age of fifty-four, I finally learned my lesson!

YOU CAN'T DEFINE WHAT YOU DON'T SEE

I have often taught that people change only when they hurt enough that they have to, learn enough that they want to, or receive enough that they are able to. In my case, pain prompted me to learn. In 2001, I came face-to-face with a painful reality: one of my companies was steadily losing money and its efforts seemed to be going in too many directions. This problem did not appear suddenly. For five years there had been indicators that I should make changes, but I was unwilling to make them. I needed to change my leadership team, but I didn't want to do it. I loved my inner circle. And year after year, I was willing to absorb the small losses that the company experienced. But after five years, the losses began to add up and take their toll.

My brother, Larry, who excels in business and always has a firm grasp on reality, kept exhorting me to face the truth and make some tough decisions. As a leader, I know the first rule of winning is "Don't beat yourself." By not facing reality and making some very uncomfortable changes, I was beating myself, and I was beginning to feel discouraged. So when Margaret and I left to visit London for two weeks, I resolved to wrestle with the issues and come to some kind of decision. To help me think things through and process my decisions, I read a book that had just been published: *Jack: Straight from the Gut* by Jack Welch. In it I read the following six rules for successful leadership:

1. Control your destiny, or someone else will.
2. Face reality as it is, not as it was or as you wish it were.
3. Be candid with everyone.
4. Don't manage, lead.
5. Change before you have to.
6. If you don't have a competitive advantage, don't compete.

As I read this advice from the CEO of CEOs, I realized that five of his six rules for successful leadership were about facing reality. It was like having a bucket of cold water thrown in my face. When I returned home, I gathered my key people around me, read them the six rules, and announced the changes I would be making within the company.

For the next three years I kept Welch's six rules in my briefcase. I often pulled them out and reread them, especially when I was facing yet another difficult leadership decision.

VISION ≠ FANTASY

One of the pitfalls that can stop potential leaders is the desire to focus on vision to the detriment of facing reality. But good leaders are both visionary *and* realistic. The Law of the Scoreboard in my book *The 17 Indisputable Laws of Teamwork* states, "The team can make adjustments when it knows where it stands." In other words, reality is the foundation for positive change. If you don't face reality, then you will not be able to make necessary changes.

> *"Realistic leaders are objective enough to minimize illusions. They understand that self-deception can cost them their vision."*
> —Bill Easum

Bill Easum, president and senior managing partner in Easum, Bandy and Associates, asserts, "Realistic leaders are objective enough to minimize illusions. They understand that self-deception can cost them their vision." That was true for me. My high belief in people and my desire to protect people I loved got in the way of facing the truth—and being honest with them when their performance was hurting the company.

If you are optimistic, as I am, and you naturally encourage people, as I do, then you may need to take extra care to look reality in the eye and keep yourself grounded. Continually cast a realistic eye on . . .

- *The Situation*—it is often worse than you think.
- *The Process*—it usually takes longer than you think.
- *The Price*—it always costs more than you think.

If you lack realism today, then you may lack credibility with others tomorrow. As my friend Andy Stanley says, "Facing current reality is often nasty, but necessary."

REALITY CHECK

In *Managing in Turbulent Times*, Peter Drucker writes, "A time of turbulence is a dangerous time, but its greatest danger is a temptation to deny reality."[1] To guard myself from that danger, a few years ago I wrote the following questions. They help me handle the nasty but necessary realities of life. Perhaps they can also help you.

Questions I Ask to Help Me Define Reality

1. *What is reality in this situation?* Do others agree with my assessment?
2. *Can I identify each issue?* Can I break down reality to better understand it?
3. *Can the issues be fixed?* Separate the solvable from the unsolvable.
4. *What are the options?* Establish a game plan.
5. *Am I willing to follow the game plan?* My commitment as a leader is essential.
6. *Will my leadership team follow the game plan?* Their commitment as leaders is also essential.

These questions force me to look realistically at the issues rather than glossing over and putting a positive spin on them.

As leaders, what we do—or don't do—always has consequences. We can try to maintain an unrealistic outlook or lifestyle, but someday we will have to pay a realistic price for it. There is no avoiding it. That was the case for me. After years of losses in my company, I had to sell a sizable interest in an investment to cover them. Every cent came out of pocket. Someone once said, "You can fool some of the people all of the time and all of the people some of the time, and that should be sufficient." As a leader, I was the one who was fooled. And the worst thing was that I had done it to myself! The greatest fool is the one who fools himself.

> *"A time of turbulence is a dangerous time, but its greatest danger is a temptation to deny reality."*
> —Peter Drucker

The ability to define reality as a leader means embracing realistic thinking so that we can see the consequences of our actions further and with greater clarity than those around us. Why is that important? When you are a leader, other people are depending on you. My inability to correctly define reality in my organization ultimately hurt not only me but others. People lost jobs, teams were torn apart, dreams went unrealized, and most sadly, some friendships ended.

GUARDING AGAINST UNREALISTIC THINKING

Although I finally learned this lesson, I still do not trust myself in this area. My mental and emotional wiring will always make me want to think the best and overlook the negative. So I have to guard against this natural bent. Asking myself questions to help me define reality isn't enough. I have to do more. Here are four practices I try to follow continually:

1. Admit My Weakness

Just as a person facing a drinking problem is helped by going to an AA meeting and saying, "I am an alcoholic," I must confess to others, "I am an unrealistic person." Admitting my weakness is a first step toward recovery. You can't *define* reality if you won't *face* reality.

2. Embrace Realistic People

The old saying "birds of a feather flock together" is really true. I like to be around people who are like me. That may be a good thing when I want to have fun, but it can be a bad thing when I want to lead well. I need people to complete me, to be strong where I am weak. An effective leadership team has members who complement one another.

3. Ask for Honesty from Others

All leaders need to have a group of people around them who will tell them what they really think. They don't need a bunch of yes-men and yes-women. The only way a leader will get honest feedback is by asking for it, and by treating people well when they actually give it. However, many leaders aren't secure enough to ask for it or to respond to it without defensiveness. Sometimes we don't want to hear the truth even though we need to. The reality is that many people don't want to face reality. That's why it is a good idea to ask others to help us.

4. Invite "Fresh Eyes" to Check Me Out

It's amazing what you don't see when you are in a familiar environment. The longer I lead, the more I realize I need people who are not in my organization to look at me and my organization. I have often paid outside consultants to come in, observe, and tell me what they see. I value what they have to say.

❧

You may be thinking, *That's a lot to be doing: looking at Jack Welch's rules, asking yourself questions to define reality, using four practices to guard against unrealistic thinking! Isn't that overdoing it?* Maybe it would be overdoing it for you—but it's not for me. Because realistic thinking is an area of weakness for me, I need to come at it from a variety of angles and have more than one system to correct the way I do things.

Defining reality is the starting point for good leadership. It's like finding "You Are Here" on a map before trying to get where you're going. As Jim Collins points out in *Good to Great*, good leaders who lead great companies face reality and make changes accordingly. "You absolutely cannot make a series of good decisions without first confronting the brutal facts."[2] Never forget, the way you define reality determines where and how you lead. And where and how you lead determines where your followers end up. In other words, a lot is depending on it.

> *Good leaders who lead great companies face reality and make changes accordingly.*

APPLICATION EXERCISES

1. What kind of thinker are you? On a scale of 1 (realism) to 10 (optimism), where are you? Do you naturally think and speak in terms of best-case scenarios (as I do) or worst-case scenarios? Now ask friends, colleagues, and your spouse to rate you. If you are highly optimistic (others might call you *un*realistic), you need to create systems in your life to keep you from leading your followers in a wrong direction.

2. Who speaks truth in your life? All leaders need people around them who are willing to speak hard truths. Who will tell you what you *need* to hear? If you have people who do that, affirm them for it and ask them to continue to do so. If you don't, find some. You don't need people who will knock you down—just people who will help you stay down-to-earth.

3. Where do you need a reality check? If you are not seeing positive results in an area you are leading, use the list of questions in the chapter to help you see if you are looking at the situation realistically. Ask yourself:

- *What is reality in this situation?* Do others agree with my assessment?
- *Can I identify each issue?* Can I break down reality to better understand it?
- *Can the issues be fixed?* Separate the solvable from the unsolvable.
- *What are the options?* Establish a game plan.
- *Am I willing to follow the game plan?* My commitment as a leader is essential.
- *Will my leadership team follow the game plan?* Their commitment as leaders is also essential.

MENTORING MOMENT

Invite the people you are mentoring to ask you hard questions about the realities of your leadership. Be direct and genuine in your responses. Now turn the tables. Ask them about the realities of their current leadership situation. By asking follow-up questions and offering insights gained from your own experience, help them to sort out which things cannot be changed and which can be redefined through effective leadership. Help them talk through a plan for changing what can be changed for the betterment of the people and the organization.

9

To See How the Leader Is Doing, Look at the People

In the mid-1970s, I attended a conference where Lee Roberson was a speaker. He made a statement during a session that inspired me and changed my life. Roberson said, "Everything rises and falls on leadership." By that he meant that leaders inevitably make things better or worse for the people who follow them. Wherever you have a good leader, the team gets better, the organization gets better, the department or division gets better. And wherever you have a bad leader, everyone that leader impacts has a tougher time. Leadership makes every endeavor either better or worse.

The moment I heard that statement, I understood intuitively that it was true. That statement soon became my theme. It has been a major inspiration and motivation for me for more than thirty years. It has been the foundation of the *21 Irrefutable Laws of Leadership,* including the Law of the Lid, which states, "Leadership ability determines a person's level of effectiveness." And it has influenced how I see everything that happens around me.

The Leader Is Responsible

The more you understand leadership, the more you see how leaders impact things around them. A few years after I heard Roberson speak, along with millions of other Americans I watched Jimmy Carter and Ronald Reagan debate prior to the 1980 presidential election. Most people agreed that the debate turned on a question that Reagan asked the American people. He said,

Next Tuesday is Election Day. Next Tuesday all of you will go to the polls and stand there in the polling place and make a decision. I think when you make that decision it might be well if you would ask yourself, "Are you better off than you were four years ago? Is it easier for you to go buy things in the store than it was four years ago? Is there more or less unemployment in the country than there was four years ago?" If you answer all those questions yes, why, then I think your choice is very obvious as to who you'll vote for. If you don't agree, if you don't think that this course that we've been on for the last four years is what you would like to see us follow for the next four, then I could suggest another choice that you have.[1]

Why would that question—"Are you better off than you were four years ago?"—have such an impact? Because people understood that *their* current condition was the result of *who* their leader was. They didn't like their condition, so they changed leaders. It's what got Reagan elected. And it's why I say that to see how the leader is doing, all you have to do is look at the people. As leadership expert Max Depree says, "The signs of outstanding leadership appear primarily among the followers."

> *"The signs of outstanding leadership appear primarily among the followers."*
> —Max Depree

People often attribute the success of organizations and teams to many things: opportunities, the economy, personnel, teamwork, resources, timing, chemistry, luck. And while it's true that any of those things can come into play, the one thing all good organizations have in common is good leadership.

Have you noticed that whenever you go to a new doctor, you have to fill out forms and answer a bunch of questions? Although they may seem trivial or irrelevant, the most important questions are those dealing with your family history. Why? Your physical health is greatly determined by your parents' physical health. If one of your parents has heart disease, diabetes, or cancer, there is a high likelihood that you will someday have it too. Your health has been passed down to you.

Leadership works in a similar way. When leaders are healthy, the people they lead tend to be healthy. When leaders are unhealthy, so are their followers. People may teach what they know, but they reproduce what they are.

Recently I spoke at a conference with Larry Bossidy, the former CEO of AlliedSignal and author of *Execution*. He touched on this dynamic between leaders and followers, and spoke about the important role leaders have with their people. He said,

> The development of new leaders is not only the key to profitability, it is also very satisfying in terms of feeling like you've left a legacy, not just an income statement. The question is often asked, "How am I doing as a leader?" The answer is how the people you lead are doing. Do they learn? Do they manage conflict? Do they initiate changes? You won't remember when you retire what you did the first quarter of 1994. What you will remember, is how many people you developed.

The best leaders are highly intentional about developing their people. But good or bad, leaders always impact their people. And if you want to know whether a leader is successful and effective, don't look at—or listen to—the leader. Simply look at the people.

REVEALING QUESTIONS TO ASK ABOUT FOLLOWERS

Earl Weaver, the former manager of the Baltimore Orioles, was known for continually baiting and arguing with umpires. One of the standard questions he asked of umpires in the first few innings of a game was, "Is it going to get any better, or is this as good as it's going to get?" That's a question every leader should ask himself. Why? Because the performance of the leader will greatly impact the performance of the team.

If you want to know how you're doing as a leader (or if you want to analyze the leadership of someone else in your organization), do it by asking the following four questions:

Question #1: Are the people following?

All leaders have two common characteristics: first, they are going somewhere; second, they are able to persuade other people to go with them. In a very practical sense, the second characteristic is what separates the real leaders from the pretenders. If someone with a leadership position has no followers, then that person has a position but isn't really a leader. There is no such thing as a leader without followers!

It's important to note that having followers doesn't necessarily make individuals *good* leaders; it just makes them leaders. Pastor Stuart Briscoe tells the story of a young colleague who was officiating at the funeral of a war veteran. The dead man's military friends wanted to have some role in the service at the funeral home, so they requested that the pastor lead them down to the casket, stand with them for a solemn moment of remembrance, and then lead them out through the side door.

The young pastor did exactly that. There was only one problem: he picked the wrong door. With military precision, he marched the men into a broom closet. The whole group then had to beat a hasty, confused retreat, in full view of the mourners.[2]

When a leader knows where he is going and the people *know* that the leader knows where he is going, they begin to develop a healthy trust. This relationship of trust will grow as the leader demonstrates continuing competence. Every time a good leader makes the right moves with the right motives, the relationship strengthens and the team gets better.

> *All leaders have two common characteristics: first, they are going somewhere; second, they are able to persuade other people to go with them.*

Clarence Francis, who led the General Foods corporation in the 1930s and '40s, asserted, "You can buy a man's time; you can buy his physical presence at a given place; you can even buy a measured number of his skilled muscular motions per hour. But you can not buy enthusiasm . . . you can not buy loyalty . . . you can not buy the devotion of hearts, minds or souls. You must earn these."

As a leader, you should never expect the loyalty of others before you have built a relationship and earned trust. Demanding it up front seldom works. The loyalty of followers comes as a reward to the leader who earns it, not the one who yearns for it. The followership of the people is based not on position but on performance and motives. Successful leaders put the good of their people first. When they do this, they earn the respect of the people and their following grows. And when a leader performs first, the loyalty that follows often has no limits.

Question #2: Are the people changing?

The second question that must be asked about the people in order to know how the leader is doing has to do with whether the people are willing to make changes for the sake of progress. Progress does not occur without change. President Harry S. Truman commented, "Men make history and not the other way around. In periods where there is no leadership society stands still. Progress occurs when courageous, skillful leaders seize the opportunity to change things for the better."

Leaders are able to seize opportunities only when their people are willing to change. Much of leadership is cultivating in people a willingness to follow a leader into the unknown based on the promise of something great. That cannot occur without change. Ironically, leaders don't change people. Rather, they are agents of change. They help to create an environment that is conducive for people to make the decision to change.

> *Good leaders inspire their followers to have confidence in them. But great leaders inspire their followers to have confidence in themselves.*

How do they do this? First, they inspire others. All good leaders inspire their followers to have confidence in *them*. But great leaders inspire their followers to have confidence in *themselves*. This self-confidence lifts their morale and gives them the energy to make the kinds of changes that will take them forward and will better their lives.

The other thing effective leaders do to promote change is create an environment of expectation. Jimmy Johnson, who coached the University of Miami to a national championship and the Dallas Cowboys to two Super Bowl victories, explained the importance of creating the right environment:

My role as a head coach was to do three things: One, bring in people who are committed to being the very best; two, eliminate people who are not committed to being the very best; and three, the most important of my responsibilities, create an atmosphere where they could achieve their goals and the goals we set for our team. I wanted to put them in the right environment and delegate the responsibility so they could be the best they could be.

People will become their best only if they are changing. And they are unlikely to change unless an effective leader is present to help facilitate the process.

Question #3: Are the people growing?

Willingness to change on the part of the people can help an organization to improve, but for an organization to reach its highest potential, the people need to be willing to do more than just change. They need to keep growing.

Author Dale Galloway says, "The growth and development of people is the highest calling of a leader." I couldn't agree more. There is a lot of talk in the business community about finding and recruiting good people, and I acknowledge that it is important. But even if you find the best people you can, if you don't develop them, your competitor who *is* developing its people will soon pass you by.

> "The growth and development of people is the highest calling of a leader."
> —Dale Galloway

The responsibility of developing people falls on the leader. And that means more than just helping people to acquire job skills. The best leaders help people with more than their jobs; they help them with their lives. They help them to become better *people*, not just better workers. They enlarge them. And that has great power because growing people create growing organizations.

Walter Bruckart, former vice president of Circuit City, remarked that the top five factors of excellence in an organization are people, people, people, people, and people. I believe that is true, but only if you are helping those people to grow and reach their potential. And that's not always easy for a leader. It can exact a high price. As a leader, my success in developing others will depend upon the following:

- My high valuation of people—this is an attitude issue.
- My high commitment to people—this is a time issue.
- My high integrity with people—this is a character issue.
- My high standard for people—this is a goal-setting issue.
- My high influence over people—this is a leadership issue.

Those core principles for people development are underlined by a leader's belief in the people. If leaders don't believe in their people, their people won't believe in themselves. And if they don't believe in themselves, they won't grow. That may sound like a heavy weight of responsibility on a leader, but that's just the way it is. If the people aren't growing, it's a reflection on the leader.

Question #4: Are the people succeeding?

Basketball coach Pat Riley, who has led two different teams to NBA championships, comments, "I think the ways a leader can measure whether or not he or she is doing a good job is (1) through wins or losses, (2) through the bottom line, (3) through the subjective and objective visual analysis of how individuals are improving and growing. If individuals are getting better results, I think the whole product is improving." The bottom line in leadership is always results. Leaders may impress others when they succeed, but they impact others when their followers succeed. If a team, department, or organization isn't being successful, the responsibility ultimately falls on the leader.

> *Leaders may impress others when they succeed, but they impact others when their followers succeed.*

It's been my experience that successful people who are not naturally gifted in leadership sometimes have a difficult time transitioning from achiever to leader. They are used to performing at a high level—doing tasks with excellence, reaching their goals, achieving financially—and they judge their progress by those things. When they become leaders, they often expect everyone else to do the same, to be self-motivated. And when the people they lead don't perform as expected, they ask, "What's wrong with them?"

Leaders think differently. They understand that they have a role in their followers' achievement and that their personal success as leaders is measured by the performance of their people. If they look at the people and see that they aren't following, changing, growing, and succeeding, they ask, "What's wrong with me?" and "What can I do differently to help the team win?"

I love helping other people to succeed because I find it highly rewarding. Recently I received a note from Dale Bronner, a gifted leader that I mentor. In it he said,

> John, you have added value to me by exposing me to things I have not experienced, equipping me with resources to expand my mind, teaching me principles which serve as guardrails for my life and providing me an avenue through which I can be accountable in a mentoring relationship. John, you have provided something for my head, my heart and my hands which all make me a more valuable person to serve others.

That's the reason I lead and mentor others.

Leadership is meant to lift up others. Peter Drucker observes, "Leadership is the lifting of a man's vision to higher sights, the raising of a man's performance to a higher standard, the building of a man's personality beyond its normal limitations." In other words, what he was saying is, "To see how a leader is doing, look at the people." That's the way your people measure you. How do you measure yourself?

To See How the Leader Is Doing, Look at the People

APPLICATION EXERCISES

1. Are your people following you? Let's start at the beginning. The answers to any other leadership questions won't matter if your answer to this one is no. When you lead, do your people follow? When you have an idea, do your people buy in? If you want your team to take risks or step up to a higher level of performance, do team members respond positively? If you're not sure, try this: make a request (an appropriate one) that is outside of the authority of your leadership position. If your people won't do it, then you aren't really leading. You need to establish relationships with them and develop trust through an extended demonstration of character and competence. Get started.

2. How do you keep score? When you measure your success, do you think in terms of your personal effectiveness or your team's? If you're not sure, take a look at your annual goals, your weekly or monthly objectives, and your daily to-do list. What percentage is focused on individual achievements? What percentage is on corporate or team achievements? If your goals are primarily individual, then you have not made the shift from achiever to leader. Recast your goals and objectives on every level to reflect broader goals where your people will change, grow, and achieve success.

3. Do you believe in your people? You will not develop people if you do not believe in them. Take a look at the principles for people development and rate yourself for each item on a scale of 1 (low) to 10 (high):

- High valuation of people—this is an attitude issue.
- High commitment to people—this is a time issue.
- High integrity with people—this is a character issue.

• High standard for people—this is a goal-setting issue.
• High influence over people—this is a leadership issue.

For any principle with a score lower than an 8, write out a plan to correct the issue (attitude, time, character, goals, or leadership).

MENTORING MOMENT

The bottom line in leadership is whether the people being led are succeeding. Talk to the leaders you are mentoring about the success and morale of the people they are leading. Compare what they say to your own observations. Give them a grade in leadership based on their people's success. (If you haven't observed their people, get out and see for yourself how they're doing.) If their people aren't doing as well as they should, coach your leaders in the five principles of people development listed above.

10

DON'T SEND YOUR DUCKS TO EAGLE SCHOOL

My wife, Margaret, and I love Krispy Kreme doughnuts. When we pass a Krispy Kreme shop, we always look for the red neon "Hot Doughnuts Now" sign that tells potential customers that the doughnuts have just been made and are coming off the assembly line, hot and fresh and delicious. Although we do not allow ourselves to indulge often, occasionally we can't help but give in to temptation. If we see the red light on, one of us will say, "It's a sign from God that we should stop and buy a doughnut!"

One evening when we were approaching a Krispy Kreme shop, we could clearly see that the light was not on, but we decided to stop anyway. Much to our delight and surprise, the doughnuts were just coming off the conveyer belt, hot and gooey.

"You forgot to turn on the sign to let the customers know the doughnuts are warm and fresh," I said to the young lady who waited on us.

"Oh, I don't turn that sign on a lot of the time," she replied. "The moment I do, people come into the store and we get too busy. If I keep the sign off, it's less hectic."

I was stunned. I wondered, *Why would she think like that?* At first it didn't make sense to me. But then, as I thought about it, I realized it was a matter of her position influencing her perception. She was an employee who didn't want to be inconvenienced. Certainly if the owners had been there, they would have turned the sign on! They wouldn't be hoping for convenience—they would have the success of the whole business and all of its employees in mind.

WHY SOME DON'T SOAR

For more than three decades, I have hosted conferences and written books with the purpose of adding value to people. Experience has taught me a valuable lesson: no matter what I do or how hard I try to help people, not everyone will respond in the same way. Some people will attend a conference and their lives will start to turn around. Others will come and tune out everything I say. Some will change; some won't. That has always frustrated me. I want everyone to learn, change, grow, and get better!

I experienced a "eureka moment" not long ago when I read something by speaker and consultant Jim Rohn. The article brought me great clarity on this issue. He has given me permission to share his words with you:

The first rule of management is this: don't send your ducks to eagle school. Why? Because it won't work. Good people are found, not changed. They can change themselves, but you can't change them. If you want good people, you have to find them. If you want motivated people, you have to find them, not motivate them.

I picked up a magazine not long ago in New York that had a full-page ad in it for a hotel chain. The first line of the ad read, "We do not teach our people to be nice." Now that got my attention. The second line said, "We hire nice people." I thought, "What a clever shortcut!"

Motivation is a mystery. Why are some people motivated and some are not? Why does one salesperson see his first prospect at seven in the morning while the other sees his first prospect at eleven in the morning? Why would one start at seven and the other start at eleven? I don't know. Call it "mysteries of the mind."

I give lectures to a thousand people at a time. One walks out and says,

"I'm going to change my life." Another walks out with a yawn and says, "I've heard all this stuff before." Why is that?

The wealthy man says to a thousand people, "I read this book, and it started me on the road to wealth." Guess how many of the thousand go out and get the book? Answer: very few. Isn't that incredible? Why wouldn't everyone go get the book? Mysteries of the mind. . . .

To one person, you have to say, "You'd better slow down. You can't work that many hours, do that many things, go, go, go. You're going to have a heart attack and die." And to another person, you have to say, "When are you going to get off the couch?" What is the difference? Why wouldn't everyone strive to be wealthy and happy?

Chalk it up to mysteries of the mind, and don't waste your time trying to turn ducks into eagles. Hire people who already have the motivation and drive to be eagles and then just let them soar.

Jim's perspective explains why the worker at Krispy Kreme didn't turn on the sign, and why I was so surprised. While I was thinking about generating income and maximizing profits, she was thinking about avoiding too much work.

THREE REASONS NOT TO SEND YOUR DUCKS TO EAGLE SCHOOL

For years my problem was that I believed that if I worked hard and taught the right things, I could turn ducks into eagles. It just doesn't work. I have to admit, this has been a hard lesson for me. I place a high value on people. I sincerely believe that every person matters. And for years, I believed that anyone could learn just about anything. As a result, I repeatedly tried to send my ducks to eagle school. Here's why I no longer do that.

1. If You Send Ducks to Eagle School, You Will Frustrate the Ducks

Let's face it. Ducks are not supposed to be eagles—nor do they want to become eagles. Who they are is who they should be. Ducks have their strengths and should be appreciated for them. They're excellent swimmers. They are capable of working together in an amazing display of teamwork and travel long distances together. Ask an eagle to swim or to migrate thousands of miles, and it's going to be in trouble.

Leadership is all about placing people in the right place so they can be successful.

Leadership is all about placing people in the right place so they can be successful. As a leader, you need to know and value your people for who they are and let them work according to their strengths. There's nothing wrong with ducks. Just don't ask them to soar or hunt from a high altitude. It's not what they do.

Author, pastor, and Dallas Theological Seminary chancellor Charles Swindoll illustrates this principle in his book *Growing Strong in the Seasons of Life* when he writes,

> Once upon a time, the animals decided they should do something meaningful to meet the problems of the new world. So they organized a school.
>
> They adopted an activity curriculum of running, climbing, swimming, and flying. To make it easier to administer, all the animals took all the subjects.
>
> The duck was excellent in swimming. In fact, he was better than his instructor was! However, he made only passing grades in flying, and was very poor in running. Since he was so slow in running, he had to drop swimming and stay after school to practice running. This caused his webbed feet to be badly worn so he became only average in swimming. But "average" was quite acceptable, therefore nobody worried about it—except the duck.
>
> The rabbit started at the top of his class in running, but developed a nervous twitch in his leg muscles because he had so much makeup work to do in swimming.
>
> The squirrel was excellent in climbing, but he encountered constant frustration in flying class because his teacher made him start from the ground up instead of from the treetop down. He developed "charley horses" from overexertion, so he only got a "C" in climbing and a "D" in running.
>
> The eagle was a problem child and was severely disciplined for being

a non-conformist. In climbing classes, he beat all the others to the top, but insisted on using his own way of getting there!

All people have strengths they can use to contribute. In *The 17 Indisputable Laws of Teamwork*, I teach The Law of the Niche, which says, "All players have a place where they add the most value." Successful people have discovered their niche. Successful leaders help their people discover theirs. As a leader, you should always challenge people to move out of their comfort zone, but never out of their strength zone. If people are moved out of their strength zone, they soon won't be in any kind of zone—comfort, strength, or effectiveness.

2. If You Send Ducks to Eagle School, You Will Frustrate the Eagles

My mother used to say, "Birds of a feather flock together." That's really true. Eagles don't want to hang around with ducks. They don't want to live in a barnyard or swim in a pond. Their potential makes them impatient with those who cannot soar.

People who are used to moving fast and flying high are easily frustrated by people who want to hold them back. I heard a story about Christian Herter, the former governor of Massachusetts, when he was running for a second term in office. One day after a busy morning of campaigning and skipping lunch, he arrived famished at a church barbecue. As the governor moved down the serving line, he held out his plate to the woman serving chicken. She put one piece on his plate and turned to the next person in line.

"Excuse me," Governor Herter said, "would you mind if I have another piece of chicken?"

"Sorry," said the woman, "I'm only supposed to give one piece of chicken to each person."

"But I'm starved," the governor said.

"Sorry, only one to a customer," said the woman. The governor was a modest man, but he was also hungry, so he decided to throw his weight around.

> *As a leader, you should always challenge people to move out of their comfort zone, but never out of their strength zone.*

"Lady, do you know who I am?" he said. "I am the governor of this state."

"Do you know who I am?" the woman responded. "I'm the lady in charge of the chicken. Now, move along mister!" Herter no doubt felt like an eagle who was being asked to answer to a duck.

Bill Hybels, a wonderful friend, came down to Atlanta to spend a couple of days with me. The first morning he said, "John, let's go run on the golf course."

Bill is a runner. He's slim and fit, and he often runs five to seven miles at a stretch. I, on the other hand, am a walker. (It's possible to be fat and walk.) We compromised. We would go around the course walking uphill and running downhill.

Off we went. We made our way slowly around the course. As we were approaching the end, all I could think about was how glad I would be when we finally got back to my home and I could rest. *Just a little more,* I thought. *We're almost there.* I was tired, but I didn't want to let on to Bill.

As we finally arrived at my house, Bill said, "That was so much fun; let's do it again!" So we did—and I almost died. I don't think I want to exercise with Bill anymore. And I'm sure he doesn't want to exercise with me. He's an eagle, and I'm a duck!

3. If You Send Ducks to Eagle School, You Will Frustrate Yourself

Have you ever led people who never did rise up and fulfill your expectations? No matter how much you motivated them, trained them, provided them with resources, or gave them opportunities, they just didn't perform according to your expectations? That's happened to me many times.

Maybe they weren't the problem. Maybe you were! A familiar Mother Goose rhyme reads,

Pussy Cat, Pussy Cat, where have you been?
I've been to London to visit the queen.
Pussy Cat, Pussy Cat, what did you there?
I frightened a little mouse under the chair.

Why did the cat start chasing a mouse in London when he was there to see the queen—a once-in-a-lifetime opportunity? Because he was a cat! What else would you expect him to do?

Cats do what cats do, ducks do what ducks do, and eagles do what eagles do. If you take a duck and ask it to do an eagle's job, shame on you. As a leader, your job is to help your ducks to become better ducks and your eagles better eagles—to put individuals in the right places and help them reach their potential.

As I've said, over the years I've made the mistake of trying to turn ducks into eagles. All I did was frustrate them and myself. You shouldn't ask someone to grow in areas where they have no natural talent.

Why? Because our ability to grow and change is very different depending on whether or not we can make choices. Let me explain. In areas where we have choices, our growth potential is unlimited. Attitude is a choice. Character is a choice. Responsibility is a choice. So, for example, if I have a terrible attitude—a 1 on a scale of 1 to 10—I can improve it all the way up to a 10 by making the right choices. I can choose to have a great attitude.

In contrast, natural ability is not a choice. It's a gift. You have whatever you have. The only real choice you have is whether or not you will try to develop it. And if you do, the growth in that area will not be as dramatic. After training and mentoring people for forty years, I've found that people can improve only about two points out of ten in any given talent. Therefore, if a person is born a 3 in a given area, he may be able to become a 5, but he'll never go from a 3 to a 10. So if you have someone who is a great swimmer and loves to fly in V formation, send him to duck school. No matter how motivated or intelligent he is, he'll never become an eagle. You cannot put in something that God has left out.

Know What You're Looking For

A few years ago when I was speaking at a national Chick-fil-A conference, a restaurant manager asked me a question: "How do you develop good leaders?"

My answer was, "Find people who are potentially good leaders."

"How do you find potentially good leaders?" he asked.

"Know what potential good leaders look like," I responded. I wasn't trying to be evasive or sarcastic. As a leader, it is your responsibility to know what you're looking for. You need to know what qualities and characteristics are present in leaders who are successful in your industry. Study successful leaders. Interview people you admire. Ask them about their development process. Find out what they were like when they were just getting started. The more you know about leadership, the easier it will be to recognize a leader when you see one.

It's very important for a leader to get the right people in the organization and put them in the right positions. There are few things that a leader does that are more important than this. If you need eagles in your organization, make it your mission to search for people who possess some of the qualities you've seen in other eagles. Look high and low. If you can't find any potential eagles within your organization, search for them outside of it. In other words, if you need a great eagle, go find a potential eagle. Only then do you have the possibility of developing that person into a great eagle. Don't get a duck. No matter how much you train that person, all you'll receive is a "quack."

APPLICATION EXERCISES

1. Who have you put in the wrong place? If you are the leader of an organization, a department, or a team, then it is your responsibility to make sure people are working according to their strengths. Have you been trying to turn ducks into eagles, frustrating everyone in the process? Set aside time to take stock of the natural talents of your people. Talk to them also about their passions, hopes, and dreams. You can't lead people well if you don't know who they are.

2. Do you need to free some eagles to soar and ducks to swim? If you have held down any eagles in your organization in the past or tried to turn ducks into eagles, you will need to do two things: First, reposition them so that they work according to their strengths. Second, you will need to regain their trust. Acknowledge their natural talents, help them to develop their strengths, and show them how they can contribute to the organization.

3. Do you know what potential leaders look like? I have yet to find an organization that had all the good leaders it needed. For that reason, good leaders are always on the lookout for potential leaders. If you have done your own research on leadership characteristics, use what you've found to create a description of what you're looking for in potential leaders. If you haven't, you may want to use one of my lists. This one is taken from my book *The 360° Leader*. I've found that good leaders and potential leaders display the following characteristics:

- **Adaptability**—Quickly adjusts to change
- **Discernment**—Understands the real issues
- **Perspective**—Sees beyond their own vantage point
- **Communication**—Links to all levels of the organization
- **Security**—Does not find identity in position

- **Servanthood**—Does whatever it takes
- **Resourcefulness**—Finds creative ways to make things happen
- **Maturity**—Puts the Team Before Self
- **Endurance**—Remains consistent in character and competence over the long haul
- **Countability**—Can be counted on when it counts

If you see people who display most of these characteristics, you are probably looking at people with great leadership potential.

MENTORING MOMENT

One of the most difficult transitions for any leader is going from leader of followers to leader of leaders. Assist the people you are mentoring in making this transition by helping them to spot, recruit, and develop potential leaders. Ask them to talk through the potential of each person they lead using the above list of characteristics. Then encourage them to start investing in those with the most potential.

11

~

KEEP YOUR MIND ON
THE MAIN THING

All the lessons in this book have enabled me to grow, but of them, learning how to keep my mind on the main thing has changed my life the most. I remember well the frustration of working hard in my first leadership position as a pastor, yet knowing I was ineffective. Most of my time was spent in counseling people and taking care of minor administrative tasks. I was putting in long hours, but was seeing very little positive results. It was a very unfulfilling time.

My eureka moment came in a college classroom where I was taking a business management course. The professor was teaching the Pareto principle, also known as the 80/20 principle. As he explained its impact, my eyes were opened. He explained that

- 80 percent of traffic jams occur on 20 percent of the roads.
- 80 percent of beer is consumed by 20 percent of drinkers.
- 80 percent of classroom participation comes from 20 percent of students.
- 80 percent of the time you wear 20 percent of your clothes.
- 80 percent of the profits come from only 20 percent of the customers.

- 80 percent of problems are generated by 20 percent of the employees.
- 80 percent of sales are generated by 20 percent of the salespeople.
- 80 percent of all decisions can be made on 20 percent of the information.

What an eye opener! It meant that the best 20 percent of my activities were *sixteen times* more productive than the remaining 80 percent. If I wanted to decrease the complexity of my life and increase my productivity, then I needed to focus on my top 20 percent. That day in the classroom I realized two things: (1) I was doing too many things, and (2) the things I was doing were often the wrong things. And that is a recipe for an ineffective life!

FINDING THE MAIN THING

I immediately began to evaluate the way I was spending my time. I knew I needed to prioritize my schedule, so I started to ask myself three questions: What gives me the greatest return? What is most rewarding? What is required of me? Those were not questions I could always readily answer. Early in a career, the easiest to answer is usually the one concerning requirements. You can work from a job description if you have one. On the other hand, most people don't start getting a true sense of what gives the greatest return for their effort until they reach their thirties—sometimes even later in life. And what is most rewarding to a person often changes during different seasons of life.

As I worked, reflected, and grew, I slowly began discovering the answers to those three key questions. My guiding principle was that the purpose of all work is results. If I wanted to accomplish objectives and be productive, I needed to provide forethought, structure, systems, planning, intelligence, and honest purpose to all that I did. But I also knew that I needed to keep things simple. I had read a study of thirty-nine midsized companies stating that the characteristic that differentiated the successful companies from the unsuccessful was simplicity. The companies that sold fewer products to fewer customers, and who worked with fewer suppliers than other companies in the same industry were more profitable. Simple, focused operations brought greater results. As Warren Buffett observes, "The business schools reward difficult, complex behavior more than simple behavior, but simple behavior is more effective." By striving for simplicity, I could help myself to keep my mind on the main thing.

During this season of my life, I changed from a doer of many things to a leader of few things. Key to this transition were five decisions I made that helped me become more focused and productive.

1. I Determined Not to Know Everything

Some people believe that great leaders have all the answers. Not true. Successful leaders don't know everything. But they know people who do. If you ask me a question related to one of my organizations and I don't know the answer, I know which person in the organization does. If you ask about my profession, I may not know the answer, but with a phone call or two, I can talk to someone who can answer the question. And if you ask about the details of my life and schedule and I don't know the answer, I guarantee you there's someone who does—my assistant.

> *"The business schools reward difficult, complex behavior more than simple behavior, but simple behavior is more effective."*
> *—Warren Buffett*

The most important decision I ever made to keep me focused and to simplify my life was to hire a top-notch assistant. For twenty-four of the last twenty-seven years of my life, I have been served by two wonderful assistants: Linda Eggers and Barbara Brumagin. Their value to me has been enormous.

My assistants are the primary hub of information for my life. Everything flows to and through them. I trust them to know everything so that I don't have to. More importantly, they have learned how to sift information and grasp the most important details. Remember, only 20 percent of all information will give you 80 percent of what you need to make good decisions. When we communicate, Linda Eggers gives me the main thing, which enables me to see what to do next, helps me to know why it is important, and empowers me to bring the appropriate resources to bear on the need at hand. For leaders, it's better to know the most important things than to know everything.

If you're a leader and you don't have a good assistant, you're in trouble. That is the first and most important hiring decision every executive needs to make. If you have the right person in place, you can keep your mind on the main thing while your assistant thinks about everything else.

Taking myself out of the middle of everything lessens my personal importance to many people in my organizations, but it allows me to do that which is personally important to me. It also means that assignments are not always done "my way." But I have discovered that most things can be accomplished effectively in many ways.

2. I Determined Not to Know Everything First

Most people have a strong natural desire to be "in the know." That's why gossip magazines and tabloid newspapers sell so well. Leaders also have a strong desire to be "in the know" when it comes to their organizations. No leader likes to be blindsided. However, good leaders can't afford to be caught up in every little detail of the organization. If they do, they lose their perspective and their ability to lead. What's the solution? Deciding that it's okay not to be the first to know everything.

In any organization, problems should always be solved at the lowest level possible. If every problem must be shared with leaders first, then solutions take forever. Besides, the people on the front lines are usually the ones who provide the best solutions, whether it's on the production line, the battle line, or the breadline.

For leaders, it's better to know the most important things than to know everything.

My assistant knows just about everything that happens in my organizations before I do. Because she is the center of information for my life, she knows the good, the bad, and the ugly, and she is the person who usually communicates those things to me. That works because I trust her completely. And when she tells me bad news, I am careful not to "shoot the messenger." Taking out your frustrations on the people who bring you bad information quickly stops the flow of communication.

3. I Determined to Let Someone Represent Me

Every leader has learned to stop merely taking action to fulfill the vision and start enlisting and empowering others to take action. (People who don't learn this lesson never become effective leaders.) However, not all leaders take the next difficult step of allowing other people to stand in for them as their representative to others. Why? Because it requires an even deeper level of trust in others. If someone misrepresents you, doesn't follow through, or does something unethical in your name, it reflects on you personally and may tarnish your reputation.

Recently, an acquaintance who owns several businesses found out that a leader he hired to run a division of his organization was engaged in shady business practices. By the time he got wind of it, the man had cost him $2 million. He fired the leader—who denied any wrongdoing—but by then the company's reputation had been irreparably damaged, and it could not recover financially. On paper, the leader's credentials had been good. But his character was another matter.

Half of being smart is knowing what you are dumb at.

The decision to let others represent you requires much time and trust. It should not be given lightly. You must get to know the people in whom you place that trust, and they must earn it through seasons of proven performance. The more you invest in those people, the lower the risk and the higher the potential return. Once you reach that level of trust with people you work with, you will be freed up even more to remain focused on the main things that really matter.

I am blessed to have several people in my life who do this. Linda Eggers, my assistant, represents me in meetings, schedules my calendar, and handles my finances and correspondence. When she talks to others on my behalf, she speaks with my authority. Charlie Wetzel, my writer, communicates with my voice and ideas through the books we've worked on together. John Hull, the president and CEO of EQUIP and Injoy Stewardship services, speaks on my behalf to leaders and organizations around the world. And Doug Carter, the senior vice president of development of EQUIP, shares the vision and tells the story of EQUIP better than I do.

How do you decide if someone else can be your representative, even when the pressure is on and the stakes are high? First, you must know their heart well enough to trust their character. Second, you must have enough shared history so that they know your heart and mind. And third, you must believe in their competence. If they can do the job 80 percent as well as you would, then they're ready.

4. I Determined to Stay with My Strengths and Not Work on My Weaknesses

Half of being smart is knowing what you are dumb at. Since I went into this in-depth in the chapter "Get in the Zone and Stay There," I don't need to here. But let me say this: to be a good leader, you need to know yourself, your strengths and weaknesses. I read in the *Gallup Management Journal*,

> The most revealing discovery [about the great leaders they studied] was that effective leaders have an acute sense of their own strengths and weakness. They *know who they are*—and who they are not. They don't try to be all things to all people. Their personalities and behaviors are indistinguishable between work and home. They are genuine. It is this absence of pretense that helps them connect to others so well.[1]

I always strive to stay with my strengths. Perhaps I have learned this lesson well because it is my natural bent to focus. I do not like to tinker. I want to do something with excellence using my full concentration, or I want to delegate it. I have to admit, I am not a well-rounded person and only do a few things well. But the bottom line is that in those areas of strength, I usually get good results because I remain focused.

5. I Determined to Take Charge of What Took My Time and Attention

The final major step I took to help me keep my mind on the main thing was to take control of my calendar. This was not easy for me. I enjoy helping people, and for the first few years of my career, other people often set my agenda and filled my calendar. Then one day I realized that I couldn't fulfill my purpose if I was forever fulfilling everyone else's.

Every leader is busy. The question for every leader is not, will my calendar be full? The question is, who will fill my calendar? If you don't take charge of your schedule, others will always be in charge of you.

If you operate the way I did, you will have to change the way you choose what you do. I started my career doing the things I was taught to do in college—whether they had value or not. Then I started to do the things other people wanted me to do. As I became more proactive and sought to be successful, I did the things I saw other leaders doing. Finally, I started doing the things that *I* should do—the things that gave the greatest return and rewards.

C. W. Ceran remarked, "Genius is the ability to reduce the complicated to the simple." Keeping your mind on the main thing requires simplification. If you can simplify your life, you will become more focused, you will possess more energy, and you will experience less stress. Like every decision in life, simplification requires trade-offs. You can't do everything, and choosing to do one thing means you can't do something else. It means saying no, even to some things you want to do. But think about the alternative. If you don't choose what trade-offs you make, someone else will.

> *"Genius is the ability to reduce the complicated to the simple."*
> —*C. W. Ceran*

Once at a convention of coaches, former Green Bay Packer coach Vince Lombardi was asked about his offensive and defensive strategies for winning football games. Other coaches had just described their elaborate schemes. Lombardi, who was famous for beginning training camp each year by holding up a football and saying, "This is a football," responded, "I only have two strategies. My offensive strategy is simple: When we have the ball, we aim to knock the other team down! My defensive strategy is similar: When the other team has the ball, we aim to knock all of them down!"[2] That may sound too simple, but it really is the bottom line for winning games in the NFL.

The strategy of simplification worked for Vince Lombardi and the Packers. It has worked for me. I pass it on because I think it will also work for you.

KEEP YOUR MIND ON THE MAIN THING

APPLICATION EXERCISES

1. What kinds of things occupy your time? Take a good look at your calendar and to-do lists from the last month. Take account of how you are spending your time. For every block of time, determine how your activities could be categorized according to the following list:

- Something I was told in school that I ought to do
- Something other people want me to do
- Something I see other successful people doing
- Something I know I should be doing

Remember, your time should be spent on things that are required, bring a high return, or are highly rewarding.

2. Are you focused on strengths? Spend some time reflecting on your strengths. If you need help determining what they are, talk to others who know you well. Once you know what activities play to your strengths, then ask yourself the following questions:

- Am I doing them more or less?
- Am I developing them more or less?
- Am I bringing others around me who complement these strengths?
- Am I enlisting others who compensate for my weaknesses?

Successful people focus on their strengths, not their weaknesses.

3. Are you stuck in the middle? Are you determined to know everything that goes on in your organization or department? Do you get a thrill from being the first to know? Do you live by the motto "If you want something done right, then do it yourself"? If so, you are limiting yourself as a leader. Begin relying on other people and cultivating trust in them. If you don't already have an assistant you can rely on, then find or develop one.

MENTORING MOMENT

Take some time and try to look objectively at the people you're mentoring. In what area does each have the greatest potential to make a contribution—not just for your company or department, but in life? Share your perspective with them and ask what they are doing to keep the main thing the main thing in their work. Ask them to describe specific steps they have taken to release less productive responsibilities to others. If they haven't already done this, coach them through the process.

12

---~---

YOUR BIGGEST MISTAKE IS NOT ASKING WHAT MISTAKE YOU'RE MAKING

Recently after I taught a session on conflict, a young man came up to me during the break and said, "I'm going to start my own organization."

"Good for you," I replied.

"Yeah," he continued, "I want to build a business 'the right way.' That way I won't have to deal with any problems."

"You know," I said as he was turning to leave, "you're making the mistake of thinking you won't make any mistakes."

IGNORANCE ISN'T BLISS

When you're young and idealistic, you think you can lead better than many of the people who have led others before you. I know that was true for me. When I got started in my career, I was positive, aggressive, optimistic—and totally naive. I often led by assumption. By that I mean that in my youthful zeal, I usually took for granted that everything was fine. I didn't look for problems because I didn't expect to have any. The result? I got blindsided. Whenever that occurred, I was bewildered. *How could such a thing happen?* I would wonder.

After getting blindsided for the fourth or fifth time, in desperation I started asking experienced leaders for help. One of those leaders told me something that changed my leadership. He said, "John, the biggest mistake you can make is to not ask what mistakes you are making."

That piece of advice set my leadership journey on a new course. It was my introduction to realistic thinking—something I was not accustomed to embracing. As I examined myself, I learned some things:

- I gave little thought to what might go wrong.
- I assumed that the "right way" would be mistake-free.
- I did not acknowledge mistakes I made to myself or others.
- I was not learning from my mistakes.
- I was not helping others by teaching lessons learned from my mistakes.

If I wanted to become a better leader, I would need to change. I would have to stop making the mistake of not asking what mistake I was making.

RECIPE FOR SUCCESSFUL FAILURE

No one ever sized people up more accurately then the person who invented the pencil eraser. Everyone makes mistakes—large and small. To get maximum attention, make a big mistake. To cause maximum damage, fail to admit it! That will keep you from growing as a leader. When it comes to success, it's not the number of mistakes you make; it's the number of times you make the same mistake. If you want to learn to fail successfully and handle the mistakes you *do* make with maximum profit, then you need to do the following five things:

> *To get maximum attention, make a big mistake. To cause maximum damage, fail to admit it!*

1. Admit Your Own Mistakes and Weaknesses

Recently I was speaking to several CEOs at a conference, and I was encouraging them to be open about their mistakes and weaknesses with the people they lead. The room became very tense, and I could tell that they were resistant to my advice.

During the next break as I was signing books, the leader of a company asked to see me privately. When I could take a break, we moved away from the others and he said, "I disagree with your suggestion that we should be open to others about our failures." Then he began to tell me how important it was to put up a strong front and be totally confident in front of your people.

I heard him out, but when he was finished, I said, "You are leading others with a wrong assumption."

"What is it?" he asked with anxiety.

"You assume that your people don't know your weaknesses," I responded. "Trust me, they do. When you admit your mistakes, it is not a surprise to them; it is a reassurance. They'll be able to look at each other and say, 'Whew! He knows. Now we don't have to keep pretending!'"

> *When it comes to success, it's not the number of mistakes you make; it's the number of times you make the same mistake.*

The first step toward anticipating mistakes and learning from the ones you do make is to take a realistic look at yourself and admit your weaknesses. You can't improve as a leader if you're too busy trying to pretend you're perfect.

Former U.S. Navy captain Michael Abrashoff writes in his book *It's Your Ship*, "Whenever I could not get the results I wanted, I swallowed my temper and turned inward to see if I was part of the problem. I asked myself three questions: Did I clearly articulate the goals? Did I give people enough time and resources to accomplish the task? Did I give them enough training? I discovered that 90 percent of the time, I was at least as much a part of the problem as my people were."[1] Admitting our failures and taking responsibility for them will allow us to go to the next step.

2. Accept Mistakes as the Price of Progress

Psychologist Joyce Brothers asserts, "The person interested in success has to learn to view failure as a healthy, inevitable part of the process of getting to the top." Nothing is perfect in this life—and that includes you! You'd better start getting used to it. If you want to move forward, you're going to make mistakes.

Pro football Hall of Fame quarterback Joe Montana remarked, "As if screwing up on the field in front of millions of TV viewers wasn't enough, the Monday after every game I got to relive my mistakes—over and over again, in slow motion and with commentary from the coaches! Even when we won, we always took time to review our mistakes. When you're forced to confront your mistakes that often, you learn not to take your failures so personally. I learned to fail fast, learn from my mistakes and move on. Why beat yourself up about it? Just do better next time."

> "The person interested in success has to learn to view failure as a healthy, inevitable part of the process of getting to the top."
> —Joyce Brothers

Not everyone is willing to confront his mistakes and not take them personally. Because Montana did, he became one of the best players in the history of the NFL. His leadership and ability to handle adversity earned him the nickname "Joe Cool." Those qualities also helped him to win four Super Bowls and be named Super Bowl MVP three times. If you want to reach your potential as a leader, expect to fail and make mistakes.

3. Insist on Learning from Your Mistakes

Author and leadership expert Tom Peters writes, "From the smallest branch to the corporate level, there is nothing more useless than the person who says at the end of the day, as their own report card, 'Well, I made it through the end of the day without screwing up.'"

There are two common responses people have concerning failure. While one person hesitates because he feels inferior, the other is busy making mistakes, learning from them, and becoming superior. People can either run from mistakes and hurt themselves, or they learn from them and help themselves. People who try to avoid failure at all costs never learn and end up repeating the same mistakes over and over again. But those who are willing to learn from their failures never have to repeat them again. As Author William Saroyan observed, "Good people are good because they have come to wisdom through failure. We get very little wisdom from success."

People in leadership need to take their cue from scientists. In science, mistakes always precede the discovery of truth.

4. Ask Yourself and Others, "What Are We Missing?"

Some people expect nothing but trouble. They are pessimistic, so they don't bother to look for anything good. Others, like me, have a natural tendency assume that everything is good. But either kind of thinking can hurt a leader. Elizabeth Elliot, author of *All That Was Ever Ours*, points out, "All generalizations are false including this one, yet we keep making them. We create images—graven ones that can't be changed; we dismiss or accept people, products, programs and propaganda according to the labels they come under; we know a little about something, and we treat it like we know everything." Leaders need to be more discerning than that.

It is easy to make decisions based on what we know. But there are always things we don't know. It is easy to choose a direction based on what we see. But what don't we see? Reading between the lines is essential for good leadership. We are most likely to do that when we ask the question, "What are we missing?"

> *"Good people are good because they have come to wisdom through failure. We get very little wisdom from success."*
> —William Saroyan

Back in the 1990s during the dot com boom, it seemed that everybody wanted to get in on what looked like a great thing. At that time, the leadership team at one of my companies entertained the idea of creating a dot com company for leaders. Every time someone brought it up, there would be tremendous energy in the room. Everyone got very excited about the potential of such a venture. However, every time this issue was discussed, my brother, Larry, would ask one simple question that brought everyone back down to earth: "How do these companies generate revenue beyond initial investments?" No one had a satisfactory answer.

Is Larry a killjoy, someone who delights in shooting down others' ideas and squashing opportunities? No, he's a realist. His question was just another version of "What are we missing?" And when reality hit the dot coms, we were glad he kept asking that question.

The value of asking, "What are we missing?" is that it causes everyone to stop and think. Many people can see what's obvious. Few can see what *isn't* there. Asking tough questions causes people to think differently. Not asking questions is to assume that a project is potentially perfect and that if it's handled with care, there will be no problems. That simply isn't reality.

5. Give the People Around You Permission to Push Back

Recently I saw a sign in a high-pressure sales office that said, "Do you like to travel? Do you want to meet new friends? Do you want to free up your future? All this can be yours if you make one more mistake." Fear of making mistakes keeps many individuals from reaching their potential. Fear of being honest with leaders about the potential problems that a course of action might bring has hurt many teams. The best leaders invite the opinions of the people on their teams.

> *The value of asking, "What are we missing?" is that it causes everyone to stop and think.*

When leaders don't get input from others on their team, it can lead to disaster. Michael Abrashoff touches on this problem in *It's Your Ship*. He writes:

> The moment I heard about it [the tragic sinking of a Japanese fishing boat off Honolulu by the submarine USS *Greeneville*], I was reminded that, as is often the case with accidents, someone senses possible danger but doesn't necessarily speak up. As the Greeneville investigation unfolded, I read in a *New York Times* article that the submarine's crew "respected the commanding officer too much to question his judgment." If that's respect, then I want none of it. You need to have people in your organization that can tap you on your shoulder and say, "Is this the best way?" or "Slow down," or "Think about this," or "Is what we are doing worth killing or injuring somebody?"
>
> History records countless incidents in which ship captains or organization managers permitted a climate of intimidation to pervade the workplace, silencing subordinates whose warnings could have prevented disaster.

Even when the reluctance to speak up stems from admiration for the commanding officer's skill and experience, a climate to question decisions must be created in order to foster double-checking.[2]

Many good minds working together are always better than one working alone. Because I've learned that lesson, I've changed from someone who avoids potentially bad news to someone who invites it. For many years I've given permission to members of my inner circle to ask me hard questions and give me their opinion when they disagree with me. I don't ever want to make a mistake and then hear a team member say after the fact, "I thought that was going to be a bad decision." I want people to tell me on the front end, not after it's too late for their advice to help. Pushback before a decision is made is never disloyalty. However, questioning a decision after it's made is not what I consider to be good teamwork.

> "If a person will begin with certainties, he will end in doubts; but if he will be content to begin with doubts, he will end in certainties."
> —Sir Francis Bacon

If you lead people, then you need to give them permission to ask hard questions and push back against your ideas. That permission *must* be given to others by the leader. Too often leaders would rather have followers who turn a blind eye instead of ones who speak with a blunt tongue. But if all is quiet when decisions are being considered, it probably won't be quiet after it plays out. English philosopher-statesman Sir Francis Bacon observed, "If a person will begin with certainties, he will end in doubts; but if he will be content to begin with doubts, he will end in certainties." I'd say those are the words of a leader who was willing to ask, "What mistake am I making?"

Your Biggest Mistake Is Not Asking What Mistake You're Making

APPLICATION EXERCISES

1. What is your attitude toward mistakes? Are you an optimist, a pessimist, or a realist? An optimist is afraid to look for possible problems. A pessimist is convinced there will be nothing *but* problems. Neither of these attitudes is beneficial. You must strive to be realistic. As you work this week, ask yourself, your colleagues, and your subordinates: (1) "What could go wrong?" and (2) "What are we missing?"

2. Are you owning up to your mistakes? Are your mistakes friends or enemies? The proof that leaders have embraced their mistakes and made them their friends can be determined by how often they make and admit them. Ask people who work with you to grade you on a scale of 1 (reluctant) to 10 (dedicated), regarding how willingly you own up to your mistakes. If your score is below an 8, you need to put more effort into admitting your weaknesses to other people, owning up to your mistakes, learning from them, and embracing failure as a part of success.

3. Are you getting the best ideas from your subordinates? How often do you ask the people you lead to give you their opinions on issues? How often do you include them in the information-gathering and decision-making processes? As the leader, you ultimately have the responsibility for making final decisions. The buck stops with you. However, if you are not making the most of the ideas and experiences of your people, you're limiting your leadership effectiveness. Start asking for the opinions of others today.

MENTORING MOMENT

If you are the immediate supervisor of the people you are mentoring, and they aren't taking risks and making mistakes, then you may be part of the problem. As a mentoring leader, you need to create an environment where mistakes are not only allowed, but they are encouraged and accepted as the price of progress. Create "space" for mistakes with the people you are mentoring. Identify areas where you want them to experiment or take risks, and give them an allowance for mistakes. Set an appointment for the future to meet with them to evaluate how it has changed their leadership.

13

─────────── ❧ ───────────

DON'T MANAGE YOUR TIME—
MANAGE YOUR LIFE

Early in my leadership years, I realized that my ability to maximize my time would be essential to my productivity and my effectiveness as a leader. As Peter Drucker said, "Nothing else distinguishes effective executives as much as their tender loving care of time."

Because I knew I needed to improve in this area, I attended a time-management seminar. I learned many valuable lessons that day. One of the things that struck me and that has stuck with me for more than thirty years was the analogy the presenter used to describe time. He said that our days are like identical suitcases. Even though they are all the same size, some people are able to pack more into them then others. The reason? They know what to pack. We spent most of that day learning about what to pack in the time allotted to us.

CHANGE IN PERSPECTIVE

I left that seminar with two impressions: First, time is an equal-opportunity employer; everybody gets twenty-four hours a day—no more, no less—but not everybody gets the same return on their twenty-four hours.

Second, there really is no such thing as "time management." The term is an oxymoron. Time cannot be managed. It cannot be controlled in any way. It marches on no matter what you do, the way the meter in a taxi keeps running, whether you are moving forward or standing still. Everyone gets the same number of hours and minutes every day. Nobody—no matter how shrewd—can save minutes from one day to spend on another. No scientist—no matter how smart—is capable of creating new minutes. Even with all his wealth, someone like Bill Gates can't buy additional hours for his day. And even though people talk about trying to "find time," they need to quit looking. There isn't any extra lying around. Twenty-four hours is the best any of us is going to get.

> *"Nothing else distinguishes effective executives as much as their tender loving care of time."*
> —Peter Drucker

You can't manage your time. So what *can* you do? Manage yourself! Nothing separates successful people from unsuccessful people more than how they use their time. Successful people understand that time is the most precious commodity on earth. As a result, they know where their time goes. They continually analyze how they are using their time and ask themselves the question, "Am I getting the best use out of my time?"

Even though most people would acknowledge that time is finite, I think the majority of them don't really understand its value. In his book *What to Do Between Birth and Death: The Art of Growing Up*, Charles Spezzano writes, "You don't really pay for things with money, you pay for them with time. In five years, I'll have put enough away to buy that vacation house we want. Then I'll slow down. That means the house will cost you five years—one-twelfth of your adult life. Translate the dollar value of the house, car, or anything else into time, and then see if it's still worth it."

GOOD LEADERS CANNOT BE BAD SELF-MANAGERS

People squander their time when they do things that bring them little or no positive return. That's bad enough when followers do it, because they waste their lives and squander their potential. But when leaders do it, they not only hurt themselves—they squander the potential of their people!

I've noticed that people who manage themselves poorly often are guilty of the following three things:

1. They Undervalue Their Uniqueness Doing What Others Want Them to Do

Poet Carl Sandburg advised, "Time is the most valuable coin in your life. You and you alone will determine how that coin will be spent. Be careful that you do not let other people spend it for you." As I mentioned in chapter 7, early in my career I allowed others to influence how I spent that "coin." As a result, I was busy but terribly ineffective. I was fulfilling others' expectations instead of doing what I was gifted to do!

> *"Time is the most valuable coin in your life. You and you alone will determine how that coin will be spent. Be careful that you do not let other people spend it for you."*
> —*Carl Sandburg*

As a leader, I want to make a difference. I want to make an impact. Don't you? My leadership went to a new level when I focused more on fulfilling my vision than fulfilling other's expectations. I believe I have been put on earth to do some specific things. I can't do those if I'm trying to be what others want me to be—and doing a poor job of it at that. I need to make my own unique contribution. No one else can do that for me.

People sometimes don't understand why I protect my calendar so fiercely and why I refuse some requests. I'm not just being contrary. I am very mission-minded. I know what I do well and what I don't. My time is limited, and I want to make the most of it. I won't let others put me in the box of *their* expectations. If you want to be an effective leader, you need to keep others from doing that to you!

2. They Ruin Their Effectiveness by Doing Unimportant Things

Essayist Henry David Thoreau wrote, "It is not enough to be busy. The question is, 'What are we busy about?'" How do you judge whether something is worthy of your time and attention? For years I have used this formula to help me know the importance of a task so that I can manage myself effectively. It's a three-step process:

Step One: Rate the task in terms of importance:
Critical = 5 points
Necessary = 4 points
Important = 3 points
Helpful = 2 points
Marginal = 1 point

Step Two: Decide the task's urgency regarding when it must be done:
This month = 5 points
Next month = 4 points
This quarter = 3 points
Next quarter = 2 points
End of year = 1 point

Step Three: Multiply the rate of importance times the rate of urgency. Example: 5 (critical) X 4 (next month) = 20.

I then judge when I should complete the task according to the following scale:

A = 16–25   Critical task to be finished by end of month
B = 9–15   Important task to be finished by end of quarter
C = 1–8   Low priority to be finished by end of year

One of the things you'll notice about this system is that there are no tasks that must be completed by the end of the day or week. Why? Because I am always trying to plan my time at least a month in advance. Leaders should be looking farther ahead than others in the organization. If leaders are always reacting to crises in the moment, the people and the organization will suffer.

3. They Reduce Their Potential by Doing Things Without Coaching or Training

Anything worth doing is worth doing better. I am always amazed when people try to accomplish anything without benefiting from the wisdom of someone who is ahead of them in the journey. Training, coaching, or mentoring can make a huge difference in how productive people can be with the time they have.

Robert Zemsky and Susan Shaman of the University of Pennsylvania did a study of 3,200 U.S. companies. What they found was that a 10 percent increase in spending on capital expenditures led to only a 3.8 percent increase in productivity. However, a 10 percent increase in spending for training led to an 8.5 percent increase in productivity.[1] If you want to make the most of your time, make the most of yourself. Find someone to help you improve your abilities and those of your people. As communicator and friend Zig Ziglar says, "The only thing worse than training employees and losing them is not training them and keeping them."

> *"The only thing worse than training employees and losing them is not training them and keeping them."*
>
> *—Zig Ziglar*

There really is an art to managing your life and making the most of your time. It's something you have to grow into. I don't meet many people who start out life doing it well. Most people don't ever learn it. Those who do develop it over time. Life management begins with an awareness of time and of the choices we should make to be a good steward of it. Those who do well at it do things that

- Advance their overall purpose in life—this helps them grow.
- Underscore their values—this brings them fulfillment.
- Maximize their strengths—this makes them effective.
- Increase their happiness—this gives them better health.
- Equip and coach others—this compounds their productivity.
- Add value to others—this increases their influence.

They understand that there is no such thing as time management—just life management.

Dwight Bain, a longtime friend of mine, recently sent me a story that made quite an impression on me in the area of life management. It's a parable written by Jeffrey Davis. Here's what it says:

The older I get, the more I enjoy Saturday mornings. Perhaps it's the quiet solitude that comes with being the first to rise, or maybe it's the unbounded joy of not having to be at work. Either way, the first few hours of a Saturday morning are most enjoyable.

A few weeks ago, I was shuffling toward the basement . . . with a steaming cup of coffee in one hand and the morning paper in the other. What began as a typical Saturday morning, turned into one of those lessons that life seems to hand you from time to time. Let me tell you about it.

I turned the dial up into the phone portion of the band on my ham radio in order to listen to a Saturday morning swap net. Along the way, I came across an older sounding chap, with a tremendous signal and a golden voice. You know the kind, he sounded like he should be in the broadcasting business. He was telling whoever he was talking with something about "a thousand marbles."

I was intrigued and stopped to listen to what he had to say. "Well, Tom, it sure sounds like you're busy with your job. I'm sure they pay you well but it's a shame you have to be away from home and your family so much. Hard to believe a young fellow should have to work sixty or seventy hours a week to make ends meet. Too bad you missed your daughter's dance recital."

He continued, "Let me tell you something, Tom, something that has helped me keep a good perspective on my own priorities." And that's when he began to explain his theory of a "thousand marbles."

"You see, I sat down one day and did a little arithmetic. The average person lives about seventy-five years. I know, some live more and some live less, but on average, folks live about seventy-five years.

"Now then, I multiplied 75 times 52 and I came up with 3,900 which is the number of Saturdays that the average person has in their entire lifetime. Now stick with me Tom, I'm getting to the important part.

"It took me until I was fifty-five years old to think about all this in any detail," he went on, "and by that time I had lived through over twenty-eight hundred Saturdays. I got to thinking that if I lived to be seventy-five, I only had about a thousand of them left to enjoy.

"So I went to a toy store and bought every single marble they had. I ended up having to visit three toy stores to round up 1,000 marbles. I took them home and put them inside of a large, clear plastic container right here . . . next to my gear. Every Saturday since then, I have taken one marble out and thrown it away.

"I found that by watching the marbles diminish, I focused more on the really important things in life. There is nothing like watching your time here on this earth run out to help get your priorities straight.

"Now let me tell you one last thing before I sign off with you and take my lovely wife out for breakfast. This morning, I took the very last marble out of the container. I figure if I make it until next Saturday then I have been given a little extra time. And the one thing we can all use is a little more time.

"It was nice to meet you, Tom. I hope you spend more time with your family, and I hope to meet you again here on the band."

You could have heard a pin drop on the band when this fellow signed off. I guess he gave us all a lot to think about. I had planned to work on the antenna that morning, and then I was going to meet up with a few hams to work on the next club newsletter. Instead, I went upstairs and woke my wife up with a kiss. "C'mon honey, I'm taking you and the kids to breakfast."

"What brought this on?" she asked with a smile. "Oh, nothing special, it's just been a long time since we spent a Saturday together with the kids. Hey, can we stop at a toy store while we're out? I need to buy some marbles."[2]

As I write this, I am sixty years old. If I live to be seventy-five, I will have 780 marbles left. Awareness of this fact gives me even more motivation to manage my life correctly and make the most of the time I have left. As a reminder of the finite nature of time, I keep a card with me at all times with the words of writer and naturalist John Burroughs. It says,

I still find each day too short . . .
For all the thoughts I want to think,
For all the walks I want to take,
For all the books I want to read,
For all the friends I want to see.

When you have a strong sense of purpose, enjoy life, and possess an awareness of how brief life really is, the days always seem too short. That's why you have to manage yourself effectively. Everything you do—in your career, in your personal life, and in your leadership—depends on it. That's a lesson I hope you learn earlier rather than later.

Don't Manage Your Time— Manage Your Life

APPLICATION EXERCISES

1. Are you squandering your time? Review the things you are currently doing on a regular basis. Are any of them driven by others' inappropriate expectations for you? Are some things unimportant? Or is everything you're doing driven by your priorities and strengths? If it is not, you need to change what you're doing. If your current position or profession prevents you from making changes to your activities, then consider changing your position or profession.

2. Are you getting help where you need it? If you are doing important tasks, but you are getting no help or training to improve your performance, you're not managing your time as well as you could. Take some time to figure out what you need: training, mentoring, or coaching. Stephen Covey calls this process "sharpening the axe." If your employer is willing to help you get these things, great. If not, pay for them yourself. Improving your abilities in high-priority areas is always a good investment in yourself that will pay off in the long run.

3. How do you decide how to spend your time? What criteria do you use? Do you do whatever you feel like in the moment? Do you create a daily to-do list? I want to challenge you to plan your time more effectively and to do so further ahead.

Consider the things you want to do in the coming month and the coming year. Then use the following formula to rate when to do them. For each task, multiply its importance (Critical = 5 points, Necessary = 4 points, Important = 3 points, Helpful = 2 points, and Marginal = 1 point) by its urgency (This month = 5 points, Next month = 4 points, This quarter = 3 points, Next quarter = 2 points, and End of year = 1 point). Then determine when the task should be scheduled on your calendar.

A = 16–25   Critical task to be finished by end of month
B = 9–15   Important task to be finished by end of quarter
C = 1–8   Low priority to be finished by end of year or eliminated

MENTORING MOMENT

How much targeted training or coaching are you providing to your people? Identify one specific skill-related area for each person you are mentoring where you will provide in-depth training or coaching. Create a plan for this area, and schedule regular sessions where you will pass on what you have learned. Your goal should be to make this person capable of replacing you in this area.

14

~

KEEP LEARNING TO
KEEP LEADING

Kurt, a salesman I had just met, and I were having breakfast at the Holiday Inn in Lancaster, Ohio. He leaned forward and asked me a question that would change the way I lived and led.

"John, what is your plan for personal growth?"

I was stumped. I didn't have a plan for personal growth. At the time, I didn't know that I needed one!

Not wanting to look bad, I began telling Kurt all about my work schedule. For fifteen minutes I tried to convince him (and myself) that working hard was helping me to grow and reach my potential. Isn't that the way it's supposed to happen? You work hard, you climb the ladder, and someday you "make it"?

> ~
>
> **To grow, you have to be intentional.**

My futile attempt to impress Kurt was like a plane circling an airport, waiting for clearance to land. Round and round it went until I finally ran out of gas.

"You don't have a personal plan for growth, do you?"

"No," I finally admitted, "I guess I don't."

The next thing he said was life changing.

"You know, John, people don't grow automatically," Kurt explained. "To grow, you have to be intentional."

That conversation took place in 1973, though it's as clear to me as if it happened last week. It spurred me to action. I immediately adopted a plan for growth in my life. And every year since then, I have recommitted myself to strategic, intentional growth.

For decades at conferences I've talked to people about the issue of personal growth. Sometimes I've been criticized for it. I remember a person coming up to me on one occasion and saying, "I don't like your plan for personal growth."

"That's okay," I replied. "What's your plan?"

"I don't have one," he said.

"Well, I like mine better!"

I suspect he believed that the only reason I talked about my growth plan was to sell books. What he didn't know was that I started talking about having a personal growth plan long before I ever had a book or tape to sell. I know that people don't reach their potential on accident. The secret to success can be found in people's daily agendas. If they do something intentional to grow every day, they move closer to reaching their potential. If they don't, their potential slowly slips away over the course of their lifetime.

If you want to be a good leader, you've got to be a good learner. I wrote my book *Today Matters* to try to help people with this idea. In the chapter "Defining Moments Define Your Leadership," I shared the "Daily Dozen" that I use for personal growth. It might serve you well as a personal growth track to run on. If not, find another one. The main thing is, if you don't have a plan for personal growth, then don't expect to grow!

How Will You Grow?

As you seek to learn and grow as a leader, let me give you some advice about how to approach the process. After more than three decades of dedicated, continual effort to learn and grow, I offer the following suggestions:

1. Invest in Yourself First
Most leaders want to grow their business or organization. What is the

one thing—more than any other—that will determine the growth of that organization? The growth of the people in the organization. And what determines the people's growth? The growth of the leader! As long as people are following you, they will be able to go only as far as you go. If you're not growing, they won't be growing—either that or they will leave and go somewhere else where they *can* grow.

As a young leader, I spent what felt like a lot of money on books and conferences. My wife, Margaret, and I found this very difficult because we were on a very limited income. We often delayed other important expenditures so that we could invest in ourselves. Though it was difficult, those early investments have compounded, and over the years they have given me a great return by improving my leadership.

If you want to lead, you must learn. If you want to continue to lead, you must continue to learn.

Investing in yourself first may look selfish to some of the people around you. They may even criticize you for it. But if they do, they don't really understand how growth works. When airline flight attendants explaining emergency procedures tell passengers to put their own oxygen mask on first before putting masks on their children, is that instruction selfish? Of course not! The children's safety and well-being is dependent upon their parent being able to help them. As a leader, you are responsible for your people. They are depending on you! If you're in no shape to lead well, where does that leave them?

If you look around, you can see a pattern at work in every area of life. Employees get better after their supervisor does. Kids get better after their parents do. Students get better after their teachers do. Customers get better after the salespeople do. Likewise, followers get better after their leaders do. It is a universal principle. President Harry Truman said, "You cannot lead others until you first lead yourself." That is possible only if you invest in yourself first.

2. Be a Continual Learner

When a leader reaches a desired position or level of training, there is a temptation to slack off. That is a dangerous place to be. Rick Warren, author of *The Purpose Driven Life,* says, "The moment you stop learning is the moment you stop leading." If you want to lead, you have to learn. If you want to *continue* to lead, you must *continue* to learn. This will guarantee that you will be hungry for ever greater accomplishments. And it will help you to maintain credibility with your followers.

One of the most influential people in the golf world for many years was Harvey Penick. The author of the best-selling *Harvey Penick's Little Red Book: Lessons and Teachings from a Lifetime of Golf* taught pro players such as Ben Crenshaw, Tom Kite, Kathy Wentworth, Sandra Palmer, and Mickey Wright how to improve their games. When Crenshaw won the Masters in 1995, he broke down and cried afterward because Penick, his lifelong mentor, had recently passed away.

You may be surprised to learn that Penick was largely self-taught. For decades he carried around a little red book in which he jotted down notes and observations to help him improve his game. He was a continual learner. And every time he got better, so did the people he taught. Ironically, Penick never intended to publish his notes. He simply planned to hand the book down to his son. But people convinced him to publish all the lessons he had learned over the years. As a result, people are still learning from him and benefiting from his wisdom.

In my book *Winning with People*, I write about the Learning Principle, which says, "Every Person We Meet Has Potential to Teach Us Something." Maintaining an attitude of teachability is essential for being a continual learner. Contrary to popular belief, the greatest obstacle to discovery isn't ignorance or lack of intelligence. It's the illusion of knowledge. One of the great dangers of life is believing that you have arrived. If that happens to you, you're done growing.

> *The greatest obstacle to discovery isn't ignorance or lack of intelligence. It's the illusion of knowledge.*

Successful people don't see learning or achievement as a fixed destination to head for, and, having arrived, to settle into—completed and finished. Not once have I heard someone who was a continual learner talk about looking forward to coming to the end of life's challenges. They continue to exhibit an excitement, a curiosity, or a sense of wonder. One of their most engaging characteristics is their infectious desire to keep moving into the future, generating new challenges, and living with a sense that there is more to learn and accomplish. They understand that you can't conquer the world by staying in a safe harbor.

What kind of attitude do you have when it comes to learning? I've observed that people fall into one of these categories. They live in one of three zones:

- **The Challenge Zone:** "I attempt to do what I haven't done before."
- **The Comfort Zone:** "I do what I already know I can do."
- **The Coasting Zone:** "I don't even do what I've done before."

Everyone starts out in the challenge zone. As small babies, we have to learn to eat, talk, and walk. Then we go to school and keep learning. But there comes a time in every person's life when they no longer *have* to keep trying new things. This is a pivotal time. For some people it occurs pretty early in life. For others, it comes after they achieve some degree of success. That's when they decide which zone they will live in: the challenge zone, where they will continue to try new things, explore—and sometimes fail; the comfort zone, where they no longer take risks; or the coasting zone, where they don't even try anymore. It's a sad day when a person chooses to leave the challenge zone and stop growing. As Philips Brooks, the minister who spoke at Abraham Lincoln's funeral, asserted, "Sad is the day for any man when he becomes absolutely satisfied with the life he is living, the thoughts that he is thinking and the deeds that he is doing; when there ceases to be forever beating at the doors of his soul a desire to do something larger which he seeks and knows he was meant and intended to do."

There is no substitute for continual learning. Over the years I have developed a highly disciplined growth regimen:

I **read** daily to grow in my personal life.
I **listen** daily to broaden my perspective.
I **think** daily to apply what I learn.
I **file** daily to preserve what I learn.

I try to embrace the advice of German philosopher Goethe, who said, "Never let a day pass without looking at some perfect work of art, hearing some great piece of music and reading, in part, some great book."

Adopting this kind of regimen required me to change my mind-set. During the first few years I was in leadership, I wanted to be "Mr. Answer Man"—the expert others could come to for answers. After my conversation with Kurt in 1973, I wanted to become "Mr. Open Man"— someone with a teachable attitude who desired

> *"Leadership and learning are indispensable of each other."*
> *—John F. Kennedy*

to grow every day. My desire is to keep growing and learning until the day I die, not only for my own benefit, but for the benefit of others. I can never afford to forget what President John F. Kennedy said: "Leadership and learning are indispensable of each other."

3. Create a Growth Environment for the People You Lead

Soon after I dedicated myself to being a growing person, I came to the realization that most working environments are not conducive to growth. Many of my friends did not want to keep growing. In their minds, they had paid their dues by attending and graduating from college. As far as they were concerned, they knew enough. They were done. In many ways, they were like the little girl who thought that she had exhausted mathematics when she had learned the twelve times tables. When her grandfather said with a twinkle in his eye, "What's thirteen times thirteen?" she scoffed, "Don't be silly, Grandpa, there's no such thing."

The average person will try to pull down anyone around him who is working to rise above average. The road to success is uphill all the way, and most people are not willing to pay the price. Many people would rather deal with old problems than find new solutions. To be a lifelong learner, I had to get out of a stagnant environment and distance myself from people who had no desire to grow. I sought out places where growth was valued and people were growing. It helped me to change and grow—especially in the beginning of my journey.

If you are investing in yourself and have adopted the attitude of a continual learner, you may think you've done all you need to do in the area of personal growth. But as a leader, you have one more responsibility. You need to create a positive growth environment for the people you lead. If you don't, the people in your organization who want to grow will find it difficult to do so, and they will eventually seek out other opportunities.

What does a growth environment look like? I believe it has ten characteristics. It is a place where the following things occur:

- Others are ahead of you.
- You are continually challenged.
- Your focus is forward.
- The atmosphere is affirming.
- You are often out of your comfort zone.
- You wake up excited.
- Failure is not your enemy.
- Others are growing.
- People desire change.
- Growth is modeled and expected.

If you can create a growth environment, not only will the people in your organization grow and improve, but people with great potential will knock down your doors to become part of your team! It will transform your organization.

THE PEOPLE DIFFERENCE

Walt Disney remarked, "I am a part of all that I have met." Whether you are trying to cross over into the ranks of continual learners or you are trying to build an organization that possesses a growth environment, the secret to success can be found in the people who surround you. People's attitudes and actions rub off on one another.

My father loves to tell the story of the man who tried to enter his mule in the Kentucky Derby. He was immediately rejected and rebuked.

"Your mule has no chance of winning a race against thoroughbreds," the race organizers chided.

"I know," the man replied, "but I thought the associations would do him some good."

Being around people who are better than we are has a tendency to make us stretch and improve ourselves. That is not always comfortable, but it is always profitable. It's said that whenever the great poet Emerson saw the great essayist Thoreau, they would ask each other: "What has become clearer to you since last we met?" Each wanted to know what the other was learning. Great people desire to bring out the greatness in others. Small people will try to put the same limits on you that they have put on themselves.

I have Kurt to thank for helping me understand the value of growth so early in my career. Within a year of my conversation with him, I could tell that I was learning, growing, and changing. It's said that the Tartar tribes of Central Asia used to have a curse that they would use on their enemies. They didn't tell them to get lost or to drop dead. Instead they would say, "May you stay in one place forever." What a horrible thought! Can you imagine? I can't.

To see a video clip of John Maxwell teaching more on this leadership principle and to access additional helpful tools and information, visit www.johnmaxwell.com/leadershipgold.

APPLICATION EXERCISES

1. Do you have destination disease? If you think you have arrived (or can someday arrive) by achieving a certain position, acquiring a particular degree or credential, or earning a certain level of income, then you are in danger of finding yourself in either the comfort or coasting zone. What are you doing to guard against that? Make sure that your long-term personal goals are growth oriented instead of destination oriented.

2. What is your plan? Let me be the Kurt in your life by asking the question, "What is your plan for personal growth?" Working hard and putting in long hours does not ensure growth. Neither does promotion. What will you do this week, this month, and this year to actively grow. I would recommend that you read a *minimum* of one growth-oriented book a month and listen to a *minimum* of one growth-oriented CD or tape a month. In addition, schedule yourself for an annual conference or growth-oriented retreat.

3. Are you creating a growth environment? If you possess any kind of leadership position, you are responsible for creating a growth environment for the people who work for you. Use the guidelines from the chapter to start creating one. Remember, a growth environment is one in which

- Others are ahead of them (this means *you* are growing).
- They are continually challenged.
- The focus is forward (on the future, not past mistakes).
- The atmosphere is affirming.
- They are often out of their comfort zone (but not their strength zone).
- They wake up excited (they are excited about coming to work).
- Failure is not their enemy (they are allowed to take risks).
- Others are growing (you must place a high value on growth for everyone).
- People desire change.
- Growth is modeled and expected (by you and others).

MENTORING MOMENT

By taking people through this book and mentoring them, you are already making an investment in them and helping to create a growth environment. Take your investment to the next level by helping the people you're mentoring to create a personal-growth plan tailored specifically for them. Help them select the books and lessons they will use in the coming year. Send them to the conference that you believe will help them the most. And give them a personal retreat day to reflect on what they've learned and how they want to keep growing.

15

---~---

LEADERS DISTINGUISH
THEMSELVES DURING
TOUGH TIMES

What is your current goal as a leader? During the first year of my leadership career, my goal was simple: at the end of the year, I wanted to receive a unanimous vote of support at the annual business meeting of my small congregation.

I'm a third-generation minister. I grew up in a denomination where people believed that the job of a pastor was to make everybody happy. The leaders who were given the most respect in the denomination were those who never rocked the boat and who managed to keep everything calm in their organization. The more things stayed the same, the happier the people were. And they confirmed their happiness at the annual business meeting where one of the things they voted on was whether to let the pastor keep his job. To me in that first year, the greatest possible sign of my success would be a unanimous vote of approval for my leadership. That's why it was my goal.

As that first congregational meeting approached, I was quite confident that I would receive a unanimous vote. After all, I had spent an entire year doing everything in my power to please everybody at the church. At the end of the meeting when we had finished all the business and the votes had been counted, the secretary stood and read the tally: 31 yeses, 1 no, and 1 abstention. Though I tried to hide it, I was shocked, confused, and deeply hurt.

Immediately after adjourning the meeting, I hurried home and called my father who was a leader in our denomination. I told him the whole story, and numbly recounted the results of the vote.

"Dad, should I resign because of this bad vote?" I asked.

To my horror, I heard him laugh.

"No, son," he replied, "you'd better stay. I know you well, and it's the best vote you'll ever get!"

For the next six months, every Sunday morning I would look out at the people of the church and ask myself the question, "Who voted against me?" I never did find out. But I did learn something about myself. I discovered that I desperately desired the approval of others. That had the potential to be a big problem for me. Whenever an unpopular decision needed to be made, I would want to punt the ball rather than carry it. As a young leader, I was very quick to embrace the perks of leadership. I was much slower to pay the price of leadership.

When people are faced with this kind of weakness, they can run from it, or they can try to overcome it. While it is true that people should try to grow in the areas of their greatest talents, this was different. This was a *character* issue. It was the kind of weakness that threatened to short-circuit my leadership ability and derail my career. If I didn't deal with it, then I would never be effective or go to a new level as a leader.

> *As a young leader, I was very quick to embrace the perks of leadership. I was much slower to pay the price of leadership.*

What Is a Leader to Do?

It took some time, but I finally landed on a thought that would help me to make better choices as a leader during the tough times: *I can't lead people if I need people*. When I discovered this idea, I didn't mean it in an arrogant or aloof way. Of course leaders need people. The purpose of leadership is to take people where they couldn't go on their own, inspire and equip them to do what they thought they couldn't do, and accomplish what can only be done by a group working together. To do that, leaders should love their people and be close to them. However, there are times when a leader must move forward, taking a courageous step and not waiting for others' approval. It is not healthy for a leader to *need* people's approval. As a leader, if I try to please everybody, eventually I will alienate everybody. A leader must be true to the vision and the people—even when it's not popular. That is one of the burdens of leadership.

The statement "I can't lead people if I need people" became a constant reminder to me during this early season of my leadership. Every time I felt a tug of desire to please people rather than lead them effectively, I repeated the statement to myself. By the time the second annual business meeting rolled around, I was much less concerned about how the vote turned out. What mattered was that I stayed true to the vision. And by the way, my father was right. I never got a better vote. That first one was the best vote I ever had!

Making the Tough Call

Every leader faces tough times—and that's when leaders distinguish themselves and show who they really are. Leading others can be very difficult and can take great courage. Of course, it's not that way all of the time. About 95 percent of the decisions a CEO makes could be made by a reasonably intelligent high school graduate. What is often required is common sense. But CEOs don't get paid for those decisions; they get paid for the other 5 percent! Those are the tough calls. Every change, every challenge, and every crisis requires a tough call, and the way those are handled is what separates good leaders from the rest.

How do you know when you're facing a tough call and need to be at your best as a leader? You'll know when the decision is marked by these three things:

1. The Tough Call Demands Risk

I once read that as the Soviet Union overran and annexed Latvia in 1940, the U.S. vice consul in Riga was concerned that American Red Cross supplies in that city would be looted. To guard against it, he requested permission from the State Department in Washington, D.C., to place an American flag above the Red Cross flag to deter anyone from taking the supplies.

"No precedent exists for such action," the secretary of state's office cabled back.

When the vice consul received the message, he climbed up and personally nailed the American flag to the pole. He then cabled the State Department: "As of this date, I have established precedent."

Leaders have to be willing to do things others are unwilling to do. They have to put themselves on the line. Larry Osborne observed, "The most striking thing about highly effective leaders is how little they have in common. What one swears by, another warns against. But one trait stands out: Effective leaders are willing to take a risk." If you are not willing to take a risk, then you really have no business being a leader. You can't play everything safe and expect to take people forward at the same time. Progress always requires risk.

2. A Tough Call Brings with It an Inward Battle

Psychotherapist Sheldon Koop asserts, "All the significant battles are waged within self." When I think about the difficult times I have faced as a leader, I recognize that every one of them began within me—not with others. If the path were clear and smooth, it wouldn't be a tough call. And anyone could make it! In addition, any tough call you make will be questioned. It will be criticized. It will carry with it certain consequences. That's why it's a tough call.

> *"All the significant battles are waged within self."*
> *—Sheldon Koop*

Often that internal battle occurs far from the spotlight of leadership, and casual observers aren't even aware that it's happening. Pastor, author, and academician Chuck Swindoll writes, "Courage is not limited to the battlefield or the Indianapolis 500 or bravely catching a thief in your house. The real tests of courage are much quieter. They are the inner test, like remaining faithful when nobody's looking, like enduring pain when the room is empty, like standing alone when you're misunderstood." Doing the right thing isn't always easy, but it is always necessary if a leader wants to have integrity and be effective.

Because most tough calls also result in an outward battle, a leader must win the first victory on the inside. If you are unsettled internally on an issue, you will not have the security you need for the external battle. That's why I spend time making sure I am convinced about a course of action before I try to convince others. Once I am convinced of the right course of action, I have the courage to see the decision through, no matter how tough the call was or how difficult the aftermath becomes.

3. A Tough Call Will Distinguish You as a Leader

Every now and then I hear leaders complain about the difficult times they are facing in leading their organization. It makes me want to say, "Thank God for the tough times. They are the reason you are there—to be the leader. If everything was going well, the people wouldn't need you!"

> "When the right person is the leader, he does even better during tough times."
> —Rudy Giuliani

Former New York City mayor Rudy Giuliani says, "When the right person is the leader, he does even better during tough times." I think that's true. When an organization has momentum, nearly anyone can lead. All the person has to do is find out the direction the people are going and get in front of them! When there is no momentum, a good leader will give direction and encourage forward progress. But when an organization has not only lost momentum but is moving in the wrong direction, that's when leaders really earn their pay! Only the very best leaders can lead effectively in such situations. It is during those tough times that they make the toughest decisions and really distinguish themselves as leaders.

RISING TO THE OCCASION

As a leader, you need to be aware that the tough times will either make or break you. Britain's great former prime minister Winston Churchill noted, "To each there comes in their lifetime a special moment when they are figuratively tapped on the shoulder and offered the chance to do a very special thing, unique to them and fitting their talents. What a tragedy if that moment finds them unprepared or unqualified for that which could have been their finest hour." One of the keys to being prepared for your finest hour is to make the tough calls in the smaller minutes that precede it. You have to be willing to do the small things, the difficult things, the unseen things. They prepare you for the major difficulties. If you aren't willing to take care of the little difficulties, don't expect to be able to rise up to meet the big ones. But if you do well with the small ones, you will be able to distinguish yourself during the big ones. That is where you will earn your reputation.

A few years ago, I received a letter from my friend Kent Millard, who told me a story about a different kind of leader. He wrote:

In August 1999, my wife, Minnietta, and I vacationed with some friends who live in a remote part of Alaska near Denali Park. One day they took us to visit their neighbor, Jeff King, who lives a few miles away. Jeff is a sled dog racer who has won the Iditarod 1,100 mile race from Anchorage to Nome, Alaska, three times (1993, 1996, 1998). It was a joy to experience Jeff's love and passion for his seventy huskies and his admiration for their maturity, strength, and courage.

Jeff told us that when he starts the Iditarod race he starts with sixteen dogs and rotates the lead dog frequently to give all the dogs a chance to lead since every one of them wants to be the lead dog. Eventually, he finds the dog that is the real leader because it is a dog that is energetic and persistent in leading, and that dog becomes the leader of the pack. It is chosen as the leader because it leads; it is able to motivate the other dogs to follow by its own energy and enthusiasm.

Jeff told us that in 1996, the lead dog was a two-and-a-half-year-old female, which was very unusual since there were only two females in the pack and she was so young and smaller than the other male dogs. But, he said with emotion in his voice, "She was our leader; when a blizzard came, she didn't give up. She kept barking and running even when the snow was over her head and inspired us all to keep going. Even at her young age, she has the mental maturity of a leader."

When Jeff was congratulated for winning the 1998 Iditarod, he lifted up his lead dog and said, "Here is the leader who won the race for us."

No matter how tough it gets, a real leader will keep on leading and never give up. It doesn't matter what kind of storm comes. It doesn't matter how far she is in over her head.

If you haven't already had the chance to distinguish yourself by making tough calls for the sake of your people and the betterment of the organization, don't lose hope. Your opportunity will come. If you keep doing the right thing, you will continue to gain greater responsibility. And the more responsibility you have, the more tough calls you will have to make. Meanwhile, keep learning and growing as a leader. Right now you are getting ready. When the tough times come, you will get a chance to distinguish yourself as a leader. And when you do finally meet some great challenge, it can be your finest hour!

LEADERS DISTINGUISH THEMSELVES DURING TOUGH TIMES

APPLICATION EXERCISES

1. Have you made the tough calls in the past? Your track record related to tough calls has a lot to do with your current credibility and reputation as a leader. Make a list of the tough calls you made—along with the year you made them—ones that were strongly questioned and heavily criticized. What kind of pattern do you see? If you have been in leadership a long time, you should see *many* tough decisions. If not, you are not doing the hard work a leader should. Do you see a decline in the number of tough decisions over time? If so, you may be losing your edge as a leader.

2. Are you prepared to win the battle within? What do you do to win the internal battles required of every leader facing tough times? Do you have a list of values or a set of standards by which to make decisions? Do you engage in any kinds of daily disciplines that keep you mentally, emotionally, spiritually, and physically strong? When opportunity comes, it's too late to prepare. Do today what you can so that you will be ready to do tomorrow what you should.

3. Are you playing it too safe as a leader? Every tough call includes an element of risk. Are you willing to put yourself on the line if needed when making tough decisions? Are you willing to quietly make right decisions for the sake of your people or the good of the organization, even knowing you will be criticized for them? Would you be willing to sacrifice your position if that was required to maintain your values or to guard the well-being of your people?

MENTORING MOMENT

If the people you are mentoring have much responsibility, then they are probably facing tough calls right now. Ask them about the difficulties they are currently dealing with and offer to talk them though the toughest one. Encourage them to make their own decisions, and support them as you encourage them to follow through.

16

~

PEOPLE QUIT PEOPLE,
NOT COMPANIES

Many of the ideas I get for books come as the result of my experiences speaking to audiences throughout the United States and overseas. Whenever I have speaking engagements, I try to spend as much time as I can interacting with people. I chat with people during breaks and sign books whenever possible. I like meeting people, and I also like hearing their ideas and questions. For example, *The 360° Leader* came about as the result of comments I received from people over a ten-year period. I often heard comments like, "I love your leadership principles, but I can't use them, because I'm not the top leader," or "Your ideas may be good, but you have no idea how bad a leader I work for." As a result of those remarks, I wrote a book intended to help people lead from wherever they are in an organization.

As I was working on *The 360° Leader*, I often asked audiences if they ever followed a bad leader. The response was always overwhelming. An audible groan would rise from the audience, and almost everyone would raise a hand. And during one of those moments, I had a flash of insight. It seems quite obvious now, but at the time it felt like an inspiration when I asked the follow-up question, "How many have ever quit a job because of a bad leader or a bad relationship at work?" Again, almost every hand was raised. And it confirmed what I already believed to be true: people quit people, not companies.

THE DOOR SWINGS BOTH WAYS

All organizations have an influx and outflow of people that works similar to that of a revolving door. People come in through that door because they have a reason they want to be part of that company. Perhaps the vision of the organization resonates with them. Or they believe the company holds great opportunities for them. Or they value the financial and benefit package the company offers. Or they admire the company's leader. There are as many reasons as there are people who apply for a job. But when they exit the company through that door, chances are they all have something in common. Their desire to leave for "greener pastures" is often motivated by the need to get away from someone.

> *"Some cause happiness wherever they go. Some cause happiness whenever they go."*
> —Oscar Wilde

It has been my privilege to lead for-profit companies as well as nonprofit volunteer organizations. In both kinds of organizations, people come and go, but trust me—volunteer organizations are more difficult to lead. People follow you only if they want to. They don't have the incentive of a paycheck to stay or comply with anybody's leadership. The revolving door principle is truly at work with volunteers, and in some organizations, the door swings very quickly.

For more than twenty-five years I worked as a pastor, and I can tell you that people came and left all the time. Whenever it was possible, I tried to sit down and talk to anyone who was leaving the congregation. When I would ask them why they were leaving, the overwhelmingly common response was people conflict. To be honest with you, sometimes their problem was with me! Other times it was with a staff member or another volunteer. After hearing their story, I would sometimes surprise them by saying, "I don't blame you for wanting to leave. If I weren't the pastor, I would go with you!"

To be equally candid, sometimes the people who were leaving were the real problem. Some people cannot get along with anyone. Wherever they go, trouble goes with them. They are like "Bob" in my book *Winning with People*. The Bob Principle states, "When Bob has a problem with everyone, Bob is usually the problem." In those situations, I would gladly wave goodbye to Bob or Roberta and remember the words of Oscar Wilde: "Some cause happiness *wherever* they go. Some cause happiness *whenever* they go."

WHO DO PEOPLE QUIT?

As leaders, we'd like to think that when people leave, it has little to do with us. But the reality is that we are often the reason. Some sources estimate that as many as 65 percent of people leaving companies do so because of their managers. We may say that people quit their job or their company, but the reality is that they usually quit their leaders. The "company" doesn't do anything negative to them. People do. Sometimes coworkers cause the problems that prompt people to leave. But often the people who alienate employees are their direct supervisors.

Most leaders can make a good impression on employees when they first meet. Add to that the optimism people have when they start a new job. They want a new job to work out. But over time, leaders will be recognized for who they really are, not who they are trying to appear to be. If a boss is a jerk, it's only a matter of time before an employee knows it.

So what kinds of people do employees quit? Most often they come in four types:

1. People Quit People Who Devalue Them

An elderly couple, George and Mary Lou, were celebrating their golden wedding anniversary. With the divorce rate so high, a reporter wondered about their secret for success. So he asked George, "What is your recipe for a long, happy marriage?"

George explained that after their wedding, his new father-in-law took him aside and handed him a little package. Inside the package was a gold watch that George still used. He showed it to the reporter. Across the face of the watch, where he could see it a dozen times a day, were written the words, "Say something nice to Mary Lou."

All of us like to hear good things said about us. We all want to be appreciated. However, many people don't receive positive feedback and appreciation at work. Often it is quite the opposite; they feel devalued. Their bosses act superior and treat them with disdain or, worse, contempt. And that spells disaster for any relationship—even a professional working relationship.

Malcolm Gladwell, in his book *Blink*, writes about a relationship expert named John Gottman who was able to reliably predict the potential success of a couple's marriage based on their interaction with one another. What was it that he looked for that indicated that a marriage relationship was headed for disaster? Contempt. If one of the partners treated the other with contempt, the relationship was usually doomed to fail.[1]

> *It is impossible to add value to someone we devalue!*

It is impossible to add value to someone we devalue! If we don't respect someone, we cannot treat them with respect. Why? We cannot consistently behave in a way that is inconsistent with our beliefs.

It has been my observation that when leaders devalue their people, they begin to manipulate them. They start treating them like objects, not people. That is never appropriate for a leader to do.

So what is the solution? Look for people's value and express your appreciation for them. Leaders are often good at finding value in an opportunity or a deal. They need to have a similar mind-set when it comes to people. Find the value in the people who work for you. Praise them for their contribution. They may contribute value to customers with the products they produce or the services they provide. They may contribute value to the organization by increasing its overall worth. They may contribute value to their coworkers, building them up or maximizing their performance. Find something to appreciate in them, and they will appreciate working for you.

2. People Quit People Who Are Untrustworthy

Michael Winston, managing director and chief leadership officer for Countrywide Financial Corporation, says,

Effective leaders ensure that people feel strong and capable. In every major survey on practices of effective leaders, trust in the leader is essential if other people are going to follow that person over time. People must experience the leader as believable, credible, and trustworthy. One of the ways trust is developed—whether in the leader or any other person—is through consistency in behavior. Trust is also established when words and deeds are congruent.

Have you ever worked with people you couldn't trust? It's a terrible experience. Nobody likes to work with someone they can't rely on. Unfortunately, a survey conducted by Manchester Consulting indicates that trust in the workplace is on the decline. They discovered that the five quickest ways that leaders lost the trust of their people in the work place were:

- Acting inconsistently in what they say and do
- Seeking personal gain above shared gain
- Withholding information
- Lying or telling half-truths
- Being closed-minded

When leaders break trust with their people, it is like the breaking of a mirror. Strike a mirror with a stone and the glass shatters. And while it may be possible to recover all of the pieces and glue them back together, the mirror will always show cracks. The greater the damage done, the more distorted the image is. It becomes very difficult to overcome the damage done in a relationship when trust has been lost.

In contrast, the survey found that the best ways for leaders to *build* trust were to:

- Maintain integrity
- Openly communicate their vision and values
- Show respect for fellow employees as equal partners
- Focus on shared goals more than their personal agendas
- Do the right thing regardless of personal risk[2]

Building and maintaining trust as a leader is a matter of integrity and communication. If you don't want people to quit you, you need to be consistent, open, and truthful with them.

3. People Quit People Who Are Incompetent

As I mentioned at the beginning of this chapter, one of the complaints I hear most often from people is that they work for individuals who are not good leaders. Everyone wants to feel that their leader can handle the job, whether they are a worker on the factory floor, a salesperson, a midlevel manager, an athlete, or a volunteer. Leaders need to inspire confidence, and they do that, not with charisma, but with competence.

> *Leaders need to inspire confidence, and they do that, not with charisma, but with competence.*

When leaders are incompetent, they become a distraction to the team. They waste people's energy. They prevent people from keeping the main thing the main thing. They take the focus from the vision and values of the organization and place it on the behavior of the leader. If the people working for an incompetent leader have a high degree of skill, they will continually worry about the leader messing things up. If they don't have skill or experience, they won't know what to do. Either way, productivity declines, morale suffers, and positive momentum becomes impossible.

An incompetent leader will not lead competent people for long. The Law of Respect in *The 21 Irrefutable Laws of Leadership* states, "People naturally follow leaders stronger than themselves." People whose leadership ability is a 7 (on a scale of 1 to 10) won't follow a leader who is a 4. Instead, they quit and find someone else—somewhere else—to lead them.

4. People Quit People Who Are Insecure

If a leader values people, possesses integrity, and displays competence, then people will be content to follow, right? No, even if leaders possess those three qualities, there is still one characteristic that will drive people away from them: insecurity.

Some insecure leaders are easy to spot. Their desire for power, position, and recognition comes out in an obvious display of fear, suspicion, distrust, or jealousy. But sometimes it can be more subtle. Exceptional leaders do two things: they develop other leaders, and they work themselves out of a job. Insecure leaders never do that. Instead, they try to make themselves indispensable. They don't want to train their people to reach their potential and be more successful than they are. In fact, they don't want them to be able to succeed without their help. And anytime someone who works for them rises up to too high a level, they see it as a threat.

People want to work for leaders who fire them up, not who put out their fire. They want leaders who will lift them up and help them fly, not who keep them down. They want mentors who will help them reach their potential and succeed. If they perceive that their leader is more concerned with maintaining their authority and protecting their position, they will eventually find someone else to work for.

RECIPE FOR RETENTION

No matter how good a leader you are, you will occasionally lose people. That's simply a part of leadership. However, you can do things to make yourself the kind of leader that other people want to follow. Here are the things I do as I remind myself that people quit people, not companies:

1. I take responsibility for my relationships with others. When a relationship goes bad, I initiate action to try to make the relationship better.

2. When people leave me, I do an exit interview. The purpose of the interview is to discover if I am the reason they are leaving. If so, I apologize and take the high road with them.

3. I put a high value on those who work with me. It's wonderful when the people believe in their leader. It's more wonderful when the leader believes in the people.

4. I put credibility at the top of my leadership list. I may not always be competent; there are times when every leader finds himself in over his head. However, I can always be trustworthy.

5. I recognize that my positive emotional health creates a secure environment for people. Therefore I will think positively, practice right behavior toward others, and follow the golden rule.

6. I maintain a teachable spirit and nurture my passion for personal growth. I will keep learning so I can continue leading. If I keep growing, I will never become the "lid" on the potential of my people.

---◈---

It's wonderful when the people believe in their leader. It's more wonderful when the leader believes in the people.

One of the worst things that can happen to an organization is to lose its best people. When that happens, don't blame it on the company, the competition, the market, or the economy. Blame it on the leaders. Never forget—people quit people, not companies. If you want to keep your best people and help your organization fulfill its mission, then become a better leader.

APPLICATION EXERCISES

1. Can your people rely on you? Are you the kind of leader your people can trust, no matter the circumstances or conditions? Answer each of the following questions based on the findings of Manchester Consulting:

- Is there ever inconsistency between what I say and what I do?
- Do I ever seek personal gain above the shared gain of the team?
- Do I ever withhold information from my people?
- Do I ever lie or tell half-truths?
- Am I ever closed-minded?

If you answer yes to any of these questions, you have a credibility problem with your people. Begin working to remedy the situation by doing the following:

- Maintain your integrity by making your words and deeds consistent.
- Openly communicate your vision and values.
- Show respect for workers as equal partners.
- Focus on shared goals more than your personal agenda.
- Do the right thing regardless of personal risk.

The process of gaining credibility will not occur overnight. But if you consistently practice these five things, over time your people will begin to trust you.

2. What is your attitude toward your people? If you are a leader, how do you see your people?

- Are they subordinates who simply need to do what you say?
- Are they resources to be managed and manipulated?

- Are they a necessary evil to be tolerated in order to make the business succeed?
- Are they co-laborers who have a valuable and necessary role just as you do?

If your attitude is anything other than the fourth one, it isn't the positive one needed to be a successful leader. Take steps to change it. Learn more about your people, what they do, and how they contribute to the team.

3. Do you express your appreciation? It's not enough just to *think* highly of your people. You need to *express* your belief in them and *show* your appreciation for them. Take time this week to tell the individuals who follow you why you value them and to thank them for their work.

MENTORING MOMENT

Sit down with the people you are mentoring and review the turnover of workers in their area. What kinds of patterns do you see? What kinds of people have they been losing? What level of ownership do they take for their losses? Ask them to describe what they do to express value to employees, develop trust with others, increase their own competence, and develop personal security. Help them to improve in areas where they fall short.

17

---~---

EXPERIENCE IS NOT THE
BEST TEACHER

One of the most frustrating things for young leaders is having to wait to get their chance to shine. Leaders are naturally impatient, and I was no different. During the first ten years of my leadership, I heard a lot about the importance of experience. In my first position, people did not trust my judgment. They said I was too young and inexperienced. I was frustrated, but at the same time I understood their skepticism. I was only twenty-two years old.

After I led for a couple of years, people began to take notice of me. They saw that I had some ability. In my third year as a leader, a larger church considered me for their top leadership post. The position would have meant more prestige and better pay. But I soon found out that they had decided on an older, experienced leader. Once again, though disappointed, I understood.

At age twenty-five, I was nominated to become a member of my district's board. I was excited to be on the ballot. People my age were not usually considered for such a position. The election was close, but I lost to a well-respected veteran of our denomination.

"Don't worry," I was told, "someday you will sit on that board. You just need a few more years of experience under your belt."

Time after time, my youth and inexperience were pointed out to me. And I was willing to pay my dues, learn my lessons, and wait my turn. As these more experienced people passed me, I would observe their lives to try to learn from them. I looked to see what kind of foundation they had built their lives on, which influential people they knew, how they conducted themselves. Sometimes I learned much by watching them. But many times I was disappointed. There were many people with years of experience under their belts but not much wisdom or skill to show for it.

That got me to wondering: *Why had experience helped some leaders and not others?* Slowly my confusion began to clear. What I had been taught all my life was not true: experience is not the best teacher! Some people learn and grow as a result of their experience; some people don't. Everybody has some kind of experience. It's what you do with that experience that matters.

HOW WILL EXPERIENCE MARK YOU?

We all begin our lives as empty notebooks. Every day we have an opportunity to record new experiences on our pages. With the turning of each page, we gain more knowledge and understanding. Ideally, as we progress our notebook becomes filled with notations and observations. The problem is that not all people make the best use of their notebooks.

Some people seem to leave the notebook closed most of their lives. They rarely jot down anything at all. Others fill their pages, but they never take the time to reflect on them and gain greater wisdom and understanding. But a few not only make a record of what they experience; they linger over it and ponder its meaning. They reread what is written and reflect on it. Reflection turns experience into insight, so they not only live the experience but learn from it. They understand that time is on their side if they use their notebook as a learning tool, not just as a calendar. They have come to understand a secret. Experience teaches nothing, but evaluated experience teaches everything.

> *Experience teaches nothing, but evaluated experience teaches everything.*

GAINING FROM EXPERIENCE

Do you know people who have lots of knowledge but little understanding? They may have means, but don't know the meaning of anything important? Even if they have a lot of know-how, they seem to possess little know-why? What is the problem with these individuals? Their life experience is void of reflection and evaluation. When twenty-five years go by, they don't gain twenty-five years of experience. They gain one year of experience twenty-five times!

If you want to gain from your experience—to become a wiser and more effective leader—there are some things about experience you need to know:

1. We All Experience More Than We Understand

Baseball player Earl Wilson, the first black pitcher for the Boston Red Sox, quipped, "Experience enables you to recognize a mistake when you make it again." Let's face it: we're going to make mistakes. Too much happens to us in life for us to be able to understand all of it. Our experiences overwhelm our understanding. And no matter how smart we are, our understanding will never catch up with our experience.

So what is a person to do? Make the most of what we *can* understand. I do that in two ways. First, at the end of each day I try to remember to ask myself, "What did I learn today?" That prompts me to "review the page" of my notebook for the day. The second thing I do is take the last week of every year to spend time reviewing the previous twelve months. I reflect on my experiences—my successes and failures, my goals accomplished and dreams unmet, the relationships I built and the ones I lost. In this way, I try to help close some of the gap between what I experience and what I understand.

2. Our Attitude Toward Unplanned and Unpleasant Experiences Determines Our Growth

Steve Penny, head of the S4 Leadership Network in Australia, observed, "Life is full of unforeseen detours. Circumstances happen which seem to completely cut across our plans. Learn to turn your detours into delights. Treat them as special excursions and learning tours. Don't fight them or you will never learn their purpose. Enjoy the moments and pretty soon you will be back on track again, probably wiser and stronger because of your little detour."

I must admit, having a positive attitude about life's detours is a constant battle for me. I prefer the expressway and a straight route to a winding scenic road. Anytime I find myself traveling on a detour, I'm looking for the quickest way out—not trying to enjoy the process. I know that's ironic for the guy who wrote *Failing Forward*, in which I write that the difference between average people and achieving people is their perception of and response to failure. Just because I know something is true and work to practice it doesn't mean it's easy.

In 2005, my close friend Rick Goad was diagnosed with pancreatic cancer. For one year I walked beside him through the uneven experiences created by this disease. In any given week, he would hope and be afraid, ask questions and find answers, have setbacks and possibilities. He endured a lot of ups and downs.

> *The difference between average people and achieving people is their perception of and response to failure.*

This experience was unexpected for Rick because he was still a young man—only in his forties. Throughout his ordeal I watched him live one day at a time, appreciate each moment, see the silver lining in the clouds, love his friends, and spend time with his God.

More than once he said to me, "John, I would not have chosen this for my life, but I also wouldn't trade this for anything."

Rick's detour ended in his death in 2006. It was heartbreaking. But Rick taught me and everyone else around him a lot during this difficult season. By watching him, we learned about how to live.

3. Lack of Experience Is Costly

At age sixty I now look back at my youth and I cringe at my naïveté. My toolbox of experience had only one tool in it: a hammer. If all you have is a hammer, everything looks like a nail. So I pounded and pounded. I fought many battles I shouldn't have. I enthusiastically led people down dead-end roads. I possessed the confidence that only the inexperienced can possess. I had no idea how little I knew.

Harry Golden remarked, "The arrogance of the young is a direct result of not having known enough consequences. The turkey that every day greedily approaches the farmer who tosses him grain is not wrong. It is just that no one ever told him about Thanksgiving."[1] I made plenty of mistakes as a young leader, but I was fortunate. None of them was disastrous. Most of the damage was self-inflicted, and the organizations I led didn't suffer terrible consequences for my inexperience.

4. Experience Is Also Costly

Lack of experience may be costly—but so is experience. It's a fact that you cannot gain experience without paying a price. The great American novelist Mark Twain once remarked, "I know a man who grabbed a cat by the tail and he learned 40 percent more about cats than the man who didn't."

> *"I know a man who grabbed a cat by the tail and he learned 40 percent more about cats than the man who didn't."*
> *—Mark Twain*

You just have to hope that the price is not greater than the value of the experience you gain, and sometimes you cannot judge what the price will be until after you have gained the experience.

Ted W. Engstrom, former president of World Vision, used to tell a story about the governing board of a bank who chose a bright, charming, young man to succeed their retiring bank president. The young man came to the old man to ask for help.

The conversation began, "Sir, what is the main thing I must possess to successfully follow you as president of this bank?"

The crusty old man replied, "The ability to make decisions, decisions, decisions."

"How can I learn to do that?" the young man asked.

"Experience, experience, experience," replied the retiring president.

"But how do I get experience?"

The old man looked at him and said, "Bad decisions, bad decisions, bad decisions."

It is as the old saying goes: experience gives the test first and the lesson later. The acquisition of experience can be costly. But it's not as costly as not gaining experience.

5. Not Evaluating and Learning from Experience Is More Costly

It's a terrible thing to pay the price for experience and not receive the lesson. But that is often what happens with people. Why? Because when an experience is negative, people often run away from it. They're very quick to say, "I'll never do that again!"

Mark Twain had something to say on this subject too. He observed, "If a cat sits on a hot stove, that cat won't sit on that hot stove again. In fact, that cat won't sit on a cold stove either." A cat doesn't have the mental capacity to evaluate his experience and gain from it. The best he can hope to do is follow his instinct for survival. If we want to gain wisdom and improve as leaders, we need to do better than that. We need to heed the words of *USA Today* founder Allen Neuharth who said, "Don't just learn something from every experience. Learn something positive."

> *"Don't just learn something from every experience. Learn something positive."*
> —Allen Neuharth

6. Evaluated Experience Lifts a Person Above the Crowd

People who make it a regular practice to reflect on their experiences, evaluate what went wrong and right, and learn from them are rare. But when you meet one, you know it. There is a parable of a fox, a wolf, and a bear. One day they went hunting together, and after each of them caught a deer, they discussed how to divide the spoils.

The bear asked the wolf how he thought it should be done. The wolf said everyone should get one deer. Suddenly the bear ate the wolf.

Then the bear asked the fox how he proposed to divvy things up. The fox offered the bear his deer and then said the bear ought to take the wolf's deer as well.

"Where did you get such wisdom?" asked the bear.

"From the wolf," replied the fox.

Jurist Oliver Wendell Holmes said, "The young man knows the rules, but the old man knows the exceptions." That is true only when the old man has taken the time to evaluate his experiences and gain wisdom from them.

The school of life offers many difficult courses. Some we sign up for willingly. Others we find ourselves taking unexpectedly. All can teach us valuable lessons, but only if we desire to learn and are willing to reflect on their lessons. If you are, what will be the result? You may exemplify the sentiment expressed by Rudyard Kipling in his poem "If":

If you can keep your head when all about you
Are losing theirs and blaming it on you,
If you can trust yourself when all men doubt you
But make allowance for their doubting too,
If you can wait and not be tired by waiting,
Or being lied about, don't deal in lies,
Or being hated, don't give way to hating,
And yet don't look too good, nor talk too wise:

If you can dream—and not make dreams your master,
If you can think—and not make thoughts your aim;
If you can meet with Triumph and Disaster
And treat those two impostors just the same;
If you can bear to hear the truth you've spoken
Twisted by knaves to make a trap for fools,
Or watch the things you gave your life to, broken,
And stoop and build 'em up with worn-out tools:

If you can make one heap of all your winnings
And risk it all on one turn of pitch-and-toss,
And lose, and start again at your beginnings
And never breathe a word about your loss;
If you can force your heart and nerve and sinew
To serve your turn long after they are gone,
And so hold on when there is nothing in you
Except the Will which says to them: "Hold on!"

If you can talk with crowds and keep your virtue,
Or walk with kings—nor lose the common touch,
If neither foes nor loving friends can hurt you;
If all men count with you, but none too much,

If you can fill the unforgiving minute
With sixty seconds' worth of distance run,
Yours is the Earth and everything that's in it,
And—which is more—you'll be a Man, my son!

Not only will you be a man—or woman—of integrity and wisdom,
you will also benefit your people because you will be a better leader.

APPLICATION EXERCISES

1. How often do you pause to reflect on your experiences? Most leaders I know are constantly on the go. As a result, they rarely take time to stop and reflect on their experiences of the day or week. Do you carve out time to evaluate your experiences and learn from them? If you are not doing it deliberately, chances are you are not gaining from your experience, and you run the risk of having one experience twenty-five times instead of twenty-five years of experience. Plan to set aside fifteen minutes at the end of every day or an hour once a week to reflect on your experiences and learn from them.

2. How do you record what you've learned? I think people sometimes read the slogans or statements I make, such as "I can't lead people if I need people" in the previous chapter, and they think that I made them up for the book. But that is not the case. Every saying, statement, or slogan has come from the times of reflection that I have built into my life. It is a regular discipline I have practiced since I was a young man.

When life teaches you a lesson, how do you record it? Do you simply try to remember it and hope for the best? That is not a very reliable system. Begin making it a practice to write down life's lessons. You can record them in a journal. You can write them on index cards and file them away. You can put them in a computer file. Just make sure you capture them! And if you can make your thoughts creative and catchy, not only are you more likely to remember them, you will be better able to pass them on to others.

3. How do you evaluate your year? Have you ever taken time to reflect on the events of the prior year? If not, plan to do so. Set aside an entire day— or longer—to review the previous year's calendar and reflect on your experiences. Think about the best and worst things that occurred. That is where the greatest potential lessons lie. Then take time to write down what you've learned.

MENTORING MOMENT

Ask the people you're mentoring to schedule a weekly time of reflection to evaluate their experiences. For a period of time, ask them to meet with you or e-mail you monthly to give you the highlights of what they've learned. Make the contact times less frequent once you observe that they have made reflection a regular discipline.

18

The Secret to a Good Meeting Is the Meeting Before the Meeting

How do you feel about meetings? If you're like most leaders, they're not your favorite thing. I know that's true for me. I value action, progress, and results—just as most leaders do. But how often are the meetings you are asked to attend characterized by those qualities? Most meetings are about as productive as a panda mating at a zoo. The expectations for them are very high, but the results usually turn out to be terribly disappointing. As economist John Kenneth Galbraith observed, "Meetings are indispensable when you don't want to do anything."

I enjoy the story about a conference room where management put the following slogans up on the walls to try to inspire the people who would be meeting there:

Intelligence is no substitute for information.
Enthusiasm is no substitute for capacity.
Willingness is no substitute for experience.

They hastily removed the slogans after someone added their own:

A meeting is no substitute for progress.

Anyone who has spent a lot of time in meetings knows that a meeting may take minutes, but it usually wastes hours. And anytime the outcome of a meeting is to have another meeting, you know you're in trouble.

Some of the meetings that we organize and lead ourselves aren't any better. Have you ever planned a meeting only to be bushwhacked in it by the people you asked to attend? That occurred to me early in my career. In the first board meeting I held as a young leader, I went in with a plan and an agenda, and it took ninety-three seconds for the *real* leader to assume control over the meeting and take us wherever he wanted to go. The first few years I was in leadership, I felt like Gomer Pyle. Do you remember him from *The Andy Griffith Show* and later *Gomer Pyle, USMC*? Poor Gomer never had a clue. He never knew what was coming next, and when confronted with the unexpected, he'd do one of two things. Either his eyes would bug out and he'd exclaim, "Well, gaaaaaaw-ley," or he'd grin from ear to ear and crow, "Sur-prise, sur-prise, sur-prise!" I don't know about you, but I don't *want* to be a Gomer Pyle–type of leader!

Some people react to the difficulties they have with meetings by trying to surprise the attenders—but when the leader surprises the people, the people will eventually turn around and surprise the leader. Others react by becoming cynical. After serving on various committees and attending many meetings, Harry Chapman wrote up a list of rules to help him deal with the issue:

- Never arrive on time: this stamps you as beginner.
- Don't say anything until the meeting is over: this stamps you as being wise.
- Be as vague as possible: this avoids irritating others.
- When in doubt, suggest that a subcommittee be appointed.
- Be the first to move for adjournment: this will make you popular—it's what everyone is waiting for.[1]

Still others simply give up and avoid meeting altogether. But that's not a great solution. Certainly you never want to have meetings simply for the sake of having meetings, but there are times when you need to meet with people. In those times, the point of meeting is to get something accomplished. To be a good leader, you have to learn to make your meetings effective.

The Secret to a Good Meeting

Because of my frustration with meetings—especially "official" board meetings—I decided to get some advice from one of my mentors, Olan Hendrix. Over lunch I told him, "I'm getting very frustrated with trying to conduct meetings. They're not productive. People are sometimes uncooperative. And they drag on too long. How can I make my meetings more effective?"

Olan explained that meetings usually fail for two main reasons:

1. The leader doesn't have a clear agenda.
2. Other people in the meeting have their own agendas.

Either of those situations leads to surprises. "And, John," Olan summarized, "nobody likes surprises—unless it's their birthday."

"So what do I do?" I asked.

"Oh, that's simple," he answered. "Have the meeting before the meeting."

Olan went on to explain that I needed to figure out who the key people were going to be in any given meeting and have a meeting with them (individually or in small groups) beforehand to make sure we were on the same page. That way the regular meeting would go smoothly afterward. What an eye opener!

Most people are down on what they're not up on.

Most people have the wrong idea about the purpose of a meeting. I think a lot of us think of them as time savers. You pull a bunch of people into a room so that you can deliver a message once. That's the wrong way to think about a meeting. Meetings are for getting things done! To do that, you must often have a meeting before the meeting to prepare people for the meeting. Here's why:

The Meeting Before the Meeting Helps You to Receive Buy-In

Most people are down on what they're not up on. That's just human nature. They are much more positive when they are in the know. When you give people information that surprises them, their natural first reaction is often negative. If you deliver surprising news to a group of people and the most vocal and most influential react negatively, then the entire group is likely to be negative. That can take a meeting off course or bring it to a grinding halt. That's why you want to get those vocal and influential people to buy in ahead of time.

The Meeting Before the Meeting Helps Followers to Gain Perspective

What people *see* is determined by where they *sit*. They naturally see things from their own perspective, not from anyone else's, including yours. As the leader, you need to help followers see things as you do. That requires time and intentionality.

You can't shortcut the process and expect people to see things from your point of view. And leaders who want their people to follow their suggestions "just because" aren't going to get very far with that kind of positional approach. Don't surprise your people and don't expect them to pick up on everything on the fly. If you do, your people are likely to eventually dig in their heels and stop moving forward. Give influencers the right perspective before the meeting and they'll help you spread it to everyone else.

> *What people* see *is determined by where they* sit.

The Meeting Before the Meeting Helps to Increase Your Influence

Leadership is influence, nothing more, nothing less. How do you gain influence with people? You invest in them. How do you invest in them? It starts with giving them time. If the only time you spend with individuals is in meetings, and during that time you are asking them to take care of business according to your agenda, what kind of message does that send? You won't build any kind of positive relationship with people doing that. They won't feel valued. It does nothing for them, nor does it do anything for your influence.

The Meeting Before the Meeting Helps You Develop Trust

One of the most difficult responsibilities of a leader is being a change agent for the organization. Creating change requires trust from your people. When you have the meeting before the meeting, it gives you a chance to develop that trust. You can answer questions. You can more easily share your motives. You can cover details that you might not otherwise want to go into publicly. And most importantly, you can tailor the message to the individual with whom you are communicating.

The Meeting Before the Meeting Helps You Avoid Being Blindsided

Good leaders are usually pretty good at knowing what's going on. They have strong leadership intuition. They are connected to their people. They usually have a good handle on the intangibles, such as morale, momentum, culture, etc. But even the best leaders can miss something. Sometimes during the meeting before the meeting, the person they're talking to gives them information or insight that will help them avoid making a big leadership mistake.

≈

Once Olan helped me understand the importance of the meeting before the meeting, he also explained the best way to structure an official meeting to keep it on track and productive. He suggested that I set up my meetings using the following three categories for the agenda:

- *Information Items:* During this first part of the agenda, my job would be to spend a few minutes communicating what has happened in the organization since the last official meeting. These items didn't require discussion or comment.
- *Study Items:* This second part of the agenda would contain issues that were to be discussed openly and honestly. However, there was never to be any kind of decision or vote on these items at this time. At the close of discussion, a determination would be made whether the items would be put into the final category during the next meeting.
- *Action Items:* This final section contained items that required decisions. Only items that had been on the previous agenda as study items were eligible to be action items. And they would be moved to the action section only after they have been thoroughly processed.

Olan's system was eye-opening. Not only did it give me a track to run on, but if done correctly, each meeting would properly set up the subsequent meeting.

My Leadership Depended on It

As soon as Olan Hendrix acquainted me with the importance of the meeting before the meeting, I immediately began to use it, and it made a huge difference in my leadership effectiveness. And when I became the senior pastor of Faith Memorial Church in Lancaster, Ohio, in 1972, I don't think it would be an exaggeration to say that my ability to lead hinged on the use of it.

The previous leader of that church had resigned because of a bad relationship with Jim, the chairman of the board and lay leader of the congregation. When I took the position, I understood that my success as a leader would in large part be determined by my relationship with this influential person.

On my first day as the official leader of the church, I made an appointment with Jim. My agenda was twofold: (1) to take the first step in establishing a good relationship with him, and (2) to ask him for his support. We talked about a lot of things during that first meeting. Fortunately, I was able to win him over. One of the things I committed to was meeting with him before our monthly board meetings.

"There will never be any secrets or surprises," I promised. "Before I bring anything to a board meeting, I'll first bring it to you."

Jim agreed to work with me that day. And I kept my word to him. For eight years, I had the meeting before the meeting with him every month. Together we would thoroughly discuss the issues until we agreed on a course of action to recommend to the board. His support was a key to the success of my leadership, not only because he was the most influential person in the organization when I arrived, but also because he knew the history, was acquainted with all personalities, and understood everyone's hot buttons. The board meetings I led were effective because they were preceded by meetings with Jim.

Who to Meet With

The idea of having the meeting before the meeting has broader implications and applications than just sitting down with a group's most influential person before a board meeting. I have spent much of my career leading volunteers, where a leader doesn't possess the leverage of a paycheck and can't impose the threat of taking away someone's job. Volunteers follow only if they *want* to follow. As a result, leaders of volunteers are continually working to build consensus with others.

Anytime I've planned to make major changes or worked to overcome great challenges, I've had meetings before the meetings to create buy-in. Let's say, for example, I want to make a significant change that will impact the entire organization. I'll start by meeting with the board—after having the meeting before the meeting with someone like Jim.

The next group I want to meet with is the organization's top leaders. Once again, I'll have a meeting before the meeting with a key individual or two (sometimes together, sometimes separately) before that leaders' meeting. But at this point, I'm still not ready to have the organization-wide meeting. I have one more meeting before the meeting—this time with the most influential people within the organization (the top 20 percent), the movers and the shakers who get things done and influence the majority of other people in the organization. Once I've met with them and given them time to process information and buy-in, then and only then will I have the meeting with the entire organization.

> *"Good planning always costs less than good reacting."*
> —Wayne Schmidt

The bigger the project or the greater the change to the organization, the longer the process takes. It's like flying a plane—the bigger the plane, the longer the runway. It takes time to launch a big idea or to make a dramatic change.

If you're someone who leads meetings, I suggest you take the following advice:

- **If you can't have the meeting before the meeting, don't have the meeting.**
- **If you do have the meeting before the meeting, but it doesn't go well, don't have the meeting.**
- **If you have the meeting before the meeting and it goes as well as you hoped, then have the meeting!**

Having good, productive meetings is really a matter of preparation and planning. As Wayne Schmidt, a wonderful friend, once said to me, "Good planning always costs less than good reacting."

All's well that begins well. The more you prepare for the meeting before the meeting, the less time you will have to spend doing damage control after the meeting. A leader never has to recover from a good start.

During the twenty-six years that I led volunteers, all of the organizations I led were congregational. That means that all major decisions were official only with the approval of the entire congregation. (Can you imagine doing that in the corporate world?) During my career, that meant we had to deal with quite a few different kinds of issues, ranging from small decisions up to an approval for a proposed $35 million relocation. In all that time, the worst vote I ever had under my leadership was 83 percent. That is an outstanding track record in the church world. Why was my leadership so successful? It was because I listened to Olan Hendrix when I was a young leader and continually made a practice of having the meeting before the meeting. Olan's advice has the power to do similar things for you.

> *A leader never has to recover from a good start.*

The Secret to a Good Meeting Is the Meeting Before the Meeting

APPLICATION EXERCISES

1. Are your meetings structured? Many leaders don't use a set structure for meetings. As a result, their meetings often spin out of control. How do you structure your meetings? Have you planned them to get the maximum results? If not, try using the pattern outlined in the chapter: information items, study items, and action items.

2. Have you connected with the key influencer? Who is the most influential person in the key meetings you preside over? Have you connected with this individual? Do you spend time with him or her outside of meetings? If not, start having the meeting before the meeting with this person. You don't need to make any promises like I did with Jim. You may simply want to say, "Hey, can we get together? I want to discuss a couple of ideas with you."

If you've never built relationships with key individuals like this or if you've butted heads with them in the past, it may take some time and several meetings before they are willing to share their opinions. Work toward open discussion and consensus.

3. What is your plan for the next big change? If you are responsible for large organization- or department-wide initiatives, you can't afford to implement them without planning to have meetings before the meeting. Plan meetings according to levels of influence:

- Begin with individuals who influence the top positional leaders.
- Then meet with the top positional leaders.
- Then meet with the top 20 percent of influencers in the department or organization.
- Then meet with everyone in the department or organization.

Always make it part of your preparation to plan these pre-meetings, and do not move forward unless you can actually have them.

MENTORING MOMENT

Discuss with the people you're mentoring how they prepare for meetings and how they process their people through decisions and information. Talk them though a strategy for an upcoming decision and help them identify the meetings before the meetings they need to have and with whom.

19

BE A CONNECTOR,
NOT JUST A CLIMBER

When I first started out in my career, I thought leadership was a race. My goal was to prove myself and improve my ranking. I worked hard. And each year I couldn't wait as the annual report came out with the stats for every leader in our denomination. I would compare my numbers with everyone else's. I charted my progress. I checked to see whom I had overtaken. I noted which leaders ahead of me were within reach. Every year I inched closer to the top, and it gave me a great sense of satisfaction. I was climbing!

However, there were major problems with my thinking. I was working under two major misconceptions: First, I thought my leadership title made me the leader. Second, I thought that climbing the leadership ladder was a higher priority then connecting with people. The bottom line was that I didn't realize that leadership is relational as much as positional.

I had my first wake-up call when I led my first board meeting. I had the "rights" to be the leader, but not the relationships. The people in the meeting listened to me politely, but they didn't follow me. They followed Claude, a farmer who had been a part of the church since before I was born. Watching people follow based on the relationship instead of the position was at first a frustration for me. It took me nearly a decade to understand that people do not care how much you know until they know how much you care. I wish somebody had told me that sooner. Perhaps they did, but I was too busy trying to get ahead to listen. As a result, I wasn't connecting with people.

That's not to say that climbing is all wrong. You can't create progress by staying on the plateau. Leaders are naturally wired to climb. They are aggressive. They initiate. They see opportunities and seek them before others do. Most leaders are competitive, and getting to the top is part of their

Leadership is relational as much as positional.

DNA. So the question for leaders is not, should you try to get to the top? The question is, how should you try to get there? Getting to the top without connecting with our people at best allows us to lead people without their allegiance. At worst it undermines our leadership and makes it short-lived. People you climb over will look for an opportunity to pull you down.

CHANGE IN ATTITUDE

Over the years I have watched many young leaders who climbed without connecting. They placed the positional aspect of leadership ahead of the relational one, playing a form of the kid's game king of the hill—knocking down others to keep themselves on top. I think many young leaders starting out don't realize that the game of leadership can be played any other way. But there comes a point in the experience of all leaders when they become confronted with a choice. Are they going to compete at all costs, to climb over others to make sure they get to the top, or are they going to connect with others and help them if they can?

I remember well facing this decision. Early in my first pastorate, I wanted to teach my congregation how to manage their time, talents, and finances. I knew that this kind of stewardship of resources was important, but because of my lack of experience, I had no resources to draw upon to help me. I went to a bookstore in Bedford, Indiana, in search of material, and I could find *nothing*. As I drove home, I knew I could choose to give up, or I could try to develop some materials of my own. I knew it would be a very difficult and time-consuming task, but I was willing to give it a try.

It took me months to develop material out of what felt like thin air, but after a lot of extra hours of preparation, I was ready to launch my first "stewardship month." And to my great delight, it was a tremendous success! Our attendance grew, our finances increased, and people began volunteering. It was a transforming experience for our small church and a huge momentum maker. And the results could be seen in the annual report when the church's numbers jumped dramatically.

The word soon got out that something exciting had happened at our church. And it wasn't long before other church leaders were asking me to teach them how to do what I had done. In that moment, I had a dilemma. What would I do? Would I keep to myself what I had learned to myself, not sharing it with my colleagues? That way I could keep my edge and climb above many of them on the leadership ladder! Or would I share with them all that I had learned so that they could also be successful?

I'm ashamed to admit that I wrestled with this decision for many days. I really wanted to keep my advantage and continue climbing. But I finally decided not to hoard what I had. I chose to share it with others, and I started connecting. What amazed me was how fulfilled I felt after helping those leaders learn how to teach stewardship to their congregations.

For the next twenty-four years, I led an annual stewardship month with my congregations. And every year after I was done, I made my lessons available to other leaders so that they could use them too. It ended up connecting me with a lot of other leaders around the country. What's ironic is that by maintaining an abundance mind-set and sharing what I had with others, I actually climbed in reputation nationally as a leader in the area of stewardship.

That willingness to be a connector and not just a climber had other results too. In 1992, after being approached by other church leaders to help them learn how to raise funds, I started INJOY Stewardship Services. So far, the company has helped more than 3,500 congregations in the United States raise more than $3 billion!

WHICH KIND OF LEADER ARE YOU?

Most leaders naturally fall into either the climber or connector camp. They are either highly positional or highly relational. Which type of leader are you? Take a look at some of the differences between climbers and connectors:

Climbers Think Vertical—Connectors Think Horizontal

Climbers are always acutely aware of who is ahead of them and who is behind them in the standings or on the organizational chart. They are the way I was as a young leader—reading the reports to see where they rank. Moving up is very important, and the idea of moving down is terrible. Connectors, on the other hand, are focused on moving over to where other people are. They think more about who is on the journey with them and how they can come alongside them.

Positional people desire to climb the ladder; relational people are more focused on building bridges.

Climbers Focus on Position—Connectors Focus on Relationships

Because climbers are always thinking about moving up, they are often focused on their position. However, connectors are more focused on relationships. Unlike positional people who desire to climb the ladder, relational people are more focused on building bridges.

Climbers Value Competition—Connectors Value Cooperation

Climbers see nearly everything as a competition. For some, that can mean trying to win at all costs. For others it can mean seeing success as an enjoyable game. Either way, they want to end up on top. Connectors, however, are more interested in using their relationships with others to foster cooperation. They see working together as a win.

Climbers Seek Power—Connectors Seek Partnerships

If your mind-set is always to win, then you naturally want power because it helps you to climb faster and reach the top more quickly. However, climbing the leadership ladder is not really a solo endeavor. And anything you can do on your own pales in significance to things you can do with a team of people. The way to create really high-powered teams is to form partnerships, which is what connectors are more likely to do.

Climbers Build Their Image—Connectors Build Consensus

Because movement either up or down the ladder often depends on other people's perception of their performance, climbers are often concerned with their image. Their next promotion may depend on it. Connectors are more concerned with getting everyone on the same page so that they can work together.

Climbers Want to Stand Apart—Connectors Want to Stand Together

Climbers want to distinguish themselves from everybody else in the organization. Like racers, they want to create separation—to leave everyone else in the dust. Connectors, on the other hand, find ways to get closer to other people, to find common ground that they can stand on together.

◈

I have perhaps painted climbers in an unflattering light. I don't mean to do that. After all, my natural inclination is to be a climber. But success in leadership comes to those who embrace the best of both characteristics. Many climbers are relationally challenged. According to a study reported in the book *Why Smart People Fail*, the greatest problems professionals have don't relate to their competence; they relate to their relationships. A survey of two thousand employers asked them to review the reason for dismissing the last three people from their businesses. Two out of three said it was because the person they fired couldn't get along with other people.

> *If you climb without connecting, you may gain authority, but you won't have many friends.*

If you climb without connecting, you may gain authority, but you won't have many friends. A leader's goal should be to make friends *and* gain authority. So if you're a climber, you may need to temper your competitiveness and slow down to build relationships. Judith Tobin suggests the value of five qualities you may find will assist you to connect with others:

- **Appreciation** allows for differences in people and considers them interesting.
- **Sensitivity** knows about personal feelings and quickly adjusts to the moods of others.
- **Consistency** has the quality of being "real," not phony, and gives only sincere compliments.
- **Security** doesn't try to be "top dog"; it knows it isn't an automatic loss when others win.
- **Humor** laughs at itself; it is not oversensitive.

On the other hand, if you connect well but possess little desire to climb, you may end up with many friends but not much authority to actually accomplish anything. If you're a natural connector, work to increase your energy and intensify your sense of purpose and urgency. The most effective leaders always manage to balance both connecting and climbing.

THE SHIFT TOWARD CONNECTION

If you look back at the history of management and leadership ideas, you will see that over the last one hundred years, what has been valued in leadership circles has constantly shifted, and many management fads have come and gone in that time. We have moved from the ideas of John D. Rockefeller and the Standard Oil Trust to the days of Bill Gates and Microsoft. Over the course of a century, employees have worked under command-and-control practitioners: leaders who proudly swore that they didn't get ulcers; they gave them. They've functioned under management by fear, management by objectives, and participatory management.

> *If you connect well but possess little desire to climb, you may end up with many friends but not much authority to actually accomplish anything.*

But in recent years there has been a shift back to some basics that draw on ancient wisdom: having respect, developing trust, identifying vision, listening to people, sensing the environment, and acting with courage. In the sixth century BC, the Chinese sage Lao-tzu advised leaders to be selfless and to keep egocentricity in check to become more effective. He encouraged them to lead without dominating, to be open and receptive. "The wise leader," he said, "is like a midwife, not intervening unnecessarily, so that when the child is born, the mother can rightly say, 'We did it ourselves!'" That kind of a mind-set requires a more relational approach to leadership.

During the course of my career, I have changed from a climber to a connector, and I have no regrets. I can summarize the progress of my thinking in the following way:

I want to win.
I want to win, and you can too.
I want to win with you.
I want you to win, and I'll win too.

Success is fleeting—but relationships are lasting. If you take a connector's approach to leadership, you have a much better chance of succeeding, because no one ever achieved anything of significance alone. But even if you don't succeed in a given endeavor, you will have at least made some friends along the way. That not only makes the journey more pleasant, but it sets you up for success in the future. You never know how you might be able to help one another as you strive onward in leadership.

To see a video clip of John Maxwell teaching more on this leadership principle and to access additional helpful tools and information, visit www.johnmaxwell.com/leadershipgold.

Be a Connector, Not Just a Climber

APPLICATION EXERCISES

1. What is your natural inclination? Are you a connector or a climber? Use the guidelines from the chapter to help you identify your bent. Put a check next to each phrase that best describes you.

Climbers	Connectors
Think Vertically	Think Horizontally
Focus on Position	Focus on Relationships
Value Competition	Value Cooperation
Seek Power	Seek Partnerships
Build Their Image	Build Consensus
Want to Stand Apart	Want to Stand Together

2. How can you become a better connector? If you are a natural climber, you probably need to do more connecting with people. Try some of the following:

- *Walk slowly through the halls.* Take time to go through the workplace every day to connect with people relationally.
- *Remind yourself that people are human beings, not resources to be used.* Leaders sometimes dehumanize others and think of them only in terms of the mission; get to know your people and try to see things from their point of view.
- *Put someone else ahead of you.* Climbers tend to have a me-first mind-set; think of a way to put someone ahead of you in some small way every day.
- *Get off of your agenda.* Leaders have agendas—places to go, people to see, and things to do; be on the lookout for a moment in your day when you can set aside your agenda for fifteen minutes for the sake of a person-to-person connection.
- *Put the spotlight on others.* One of the ways to help you gain perspective

is to give praise and credit to others; do that at least once a day, every day.

3. How can you become a better climber? Ancient Greek historian Herodotus said, "The most hateful human misfortune is for a wise man to have no influence." If you have connections with others but no influence, then you may be wasting your potential. Increase your ability to climb by doing the following:

- *Define your purpose.* Devote some time to the strategic side of the leadership equation; know why you're there and get on purpose.
- *Sharpen your focus.* Some people-oriented individuals tend to be unfocused; if that describes you, set aside uninterrupted blocks of time to get things done without having to interact with others.
- *Pick up the pace.* Since connecting with people often requires a leader to slow down, you may be used to working at a leisurely rate; push yourself to pick up the pace.

MENTORING MOMENT

Help the people you're mentoring to see themselves for who they naturally are: climbers or connectors. Walk them through the application exercises for their type. Watch them interact with others, and give them specific pointers to help them improve in their area of deficiency.

20

The Choices You Make, Make You

Our team was finishing a weeklong book tour, and we were preparing to land in Atlanta. After visiting twenty cities in seven days, it was good to be coming home!

As the small private jet approached the runway, we were celebrating the success of the week. Then, in a moment, everything changed. The plane was hit by wind shear and dropped straight down to the runway, the wheels hitting out of balance. All conversation stopped and our eyes widened as we realized we were in danger. The pilot, without hesitation, pushed the throttle and launched the plane back into the air. In a split second we went from celebration to sober reflection. We all realized that could have been it! We sat quietly as the plane circled the airfield, and a few minutes later we landed safely.

> *Successful people make right decisions early and manage those decisions daily.*

We all applauded and now began to relax and breathe. As we got off the plane, we thanked the captain for keeping us safe. I said to him, "That was a close call. You responded so quickly to the crisis. When did you make the decision to put the plane back into the air?"

His reply amazed me: "Fifteen years ago."

He went on to explain how as a young pilot in training, he decided in advance what decision he would make for every possible air problem. "The choice was made long before the crisis," he said.

In my book *Today Matters*, I write, "Successful people make right decisions early and manage those decisions daily." Because the pilot made the decision fifteen years ago to always take the plane back up in the air, on that day with us he simply managed that previous decision. As English theologian H. P. Liddon observed, "What we do on some great occasion will probably depend on what we already are: and what we are will be the result of previous years of self-discipline." I am grateful for our pilot's discipline that day.

THE CHOICE IS YOURS

Perhaps our greatest power in life is the power to choose. Without question, choices are the most determining factor in how our lives turn out. I have often heard legendary basketball coach John Wooden say, "There is a choice you have to make in everything you do. So keep in mind that in the end, the choice you make, makes you." Some people make their lives difficult by making wrong choices. Others move through life easier because of the good choices they've made. Regardless of which road a person takes, I know this: we don't always get what we want, but we do always get what we choose.

> *"There is a choice you have to make in everything you do. So keep in mind that in the end, the choice you make, makes you."*
> —*John Wooden*

One time during a conversation with Coach Wooden, I asked him about decision making and regrets. For a few moments this ninety-six-year-old legend sat quietly in his chair thinking about the question. Then he leaned forward and said, "John, as I look back on my life, there are things I would have done differently. But if I made the best decision possible at the time I was required to make it, then I don't regret that decision." And then he concluded, "You must be true to yourself."

At age sixty, I look back on choices I have made, and I believe I have always tried to be true to myself. As a leader, I have made thousands of choices. That's something all leaders have in common. And like every leader, I have certainly made some bad choices. I wish that I could go back and have another shot at some of them. But I have always done the best I could in the moment. You can't be a good leader and follow the advice of former baseball catcher and manager Yogi Berra, who said, "When you come to a fork in the road, take it."

> *"It is our choices that show what we truly are, far more than our abilities."*
> —J. K. Rowling

When I think about the tough choices I've made, I realize three things:

1. My Choices Have Shown Me Myself

Novelist J. K. Rowling said, "It is our choices that show what we truly are, far more than our abilities." So true. If you want to know who people are, don't look at their résumés. Don't listen to what they say. Just watch what choices they make.

I may say I have certain beliefs. I may think I hold certain values. I may intend to act a certain way. But my choices reveal who I *really* am. Your choices do the same for you.

2. Many Choices Were Not Easy

Leadership is complex. By definition anytime you are out in front breaking new ground, you are in uncharted territory. There is no established track to run on. That means making choices continually.

In addition, if you are a leader, the stakes are high. The choices you make impact not only you and your family but many others. I often wish my choices as a leader were more like my experience one time on a plane when a flight attendant asked me if I wanted dinner.

"What are my choices?" I asked.

"Yes or no," she replied. Most leadership choices are not that simple.

3. The Choices I Made Changed Who I Was

I enjoy having freedom to make choices. But anyone who makes a choice needs to understand something. Once you choose, you became a servant of that choice. You must deal with its consequences, for better or worse. And that has an impact on you.

Writer and professor C. S. Lewis observed, "Every time you make a choice, you are turning the central part of you—the part that chooses— into something a little different than what it was before. Taking your life as a whole, with all your innumerable choices, you are slowly turning this central thing either into a heavenly creature or into a hellish creature." For that reason, each of us must make our choices wisely.

CHOOSING YOUR CHOICES

I have identified three critical choices that govern how I conduct myself as a leader. These choices have made me a better leader, and I believe they can do the same for you:

Choice #1: My Standards for Myself Will Be Higher Than What Others Might Set for Me

There are a lot of people in the workforce today who don't seem to maintain very high standards for themselves. Hard up for a place to eat, two salesmen stopped at a run-down restaurant on the main street of a small town. The first man ordered iced tea with his meal. The second also asked for iced tea but added, "And be sure my glass is absolutely clean!"

A few minutes later, a busboy appeared with two glasses of tea.

"Here are your drinks," he said. "Which one of you gets the clean glass?"

I have made it my goal to set higher standards for myself than others might for me because I know that a sure way to fail as a leader is to do only the bare minimum. I have been studying leaders for more than forty years. It is my observation that great leaders are never satisfied with their current levels of performance. They are not only demanding of their people, but they also continually push themselves to reach their potential. Their expectations for themselves are always higher than any standards others might set for them.

Learning from them, I have tried to adopt that same standard for my life. Why? It certainly creates better performance, but that is not the main reason. I do it because in the end, I have to evaluate my efforts and feel good about myself. The only way I know to do that is to live up to my highest potential. NBA coach Pat Riley observes, "Excellence is the gradual result of always striving to do better." If I focus on excellence and performing according to the highest possible standard, I will keep improving. It doesn't matter whether anybody else knows it or not. I know it. And when I'm tempted to slack off, I think of the words of former UCLA coach John Wooden, who advised, "Never try to be better than others, but be the best you can be."

Choice #2: Helping People Is More Important Than Making Them Happy

The decision to strive for excellence wasn't that hard for me because of the training I received from my parents. However, I found the choice to help people instead of making them happy to be much more difficult. I wanted to do both, and in the early years of my career, I often chose pleasing others over helping them. But I soon discovered that some people want what they don't need and need what they don't want. Someone has to tell them, and that task usually falls on the leader's shoulders.

> *"Excellence is the gradual result of always striving to do better."*
> —Pat Riley

The burdens of leadership are great. One of them is to be unpopular when necessary. Pulitzer Prize–winning columnist George F. Will says, "Leadership is among other things, the ability to inflict pain and get away with it . . . short-term pain for long-term gain." Because I truly did care about people, my desire to help them eventually won out over my desire to please them.

When I finally came to the conclusion that it was more important for me to help people then to make them happy, I spent some time thinking about what that would mean for my leadership. After some reflection, here is what I wrote:

Some people won't be happy when I . . .
• Uphold the mission of the organization before the wishes of the people.

- Give some people more attention then others.
- Promote some people over others.
- Attempt to move them out of their comfort zone.
- Ask them to sacrifice for the team.
- Choose the big picture over their personal picture.
- Make decisions they disagree with.

Every day as a leader I will make someone unhappy. Hopefully, their unhappiness will not be a result of my personal failures but as a result of me fulfilling my leadership responsibilities. My attitude toward those who are unhappy with me must always be right. They may at times question my ability, but never my attitude. At the end of the day I want to know that my best effort has been available to everyone.

Every day I choose to lead with an understanding of the downside of leadership. Good leaders will have critics. They will be misunderstood. Yet it is a choice I still choose to make.

Choice #3: My Focus Will Be on the Present

A friend of mine recently said to me, "John, you have no rearview mirrors in your life. You live in the present." Although some might see that as criticism, I took it as a high compliment. I make a great effort to focus on what is right in front of me. For years I had a sign in my office that read, "Yesterday ended last night." It helped me to remain focused on the present.

Many people have a tough time letting go of the opportunities they have allowed to pass them by. They spend too much of their lives recycling a junkyard of regret. They focus the best part of their lives on what might have been or what should have been. It is as if they think that if they replay it enough they can change the outcome. What a waste!

> *"Leadership is among other things, the ability to inflict pain and get away with it . . . short-term pain for long-term gain."*
> *—George F. Will*

The only thing we can control is what we do in the present. The more we replay yesterday, the further we get from today's opportunities. And the further away we move from opportunities, the tougher the road is to get back. Opportunities never look as good coming as they do going, and they wait for no one. We need to be highly attentive to spot them. And we must be focused on our present capabilities, not past regrets. Opportunities may come in many forms and they may come from any direction, but one thing is certain: they can be seen and seized only in the present.

We live in the present and that's where our strengths lie. Whatever has happened in your life has happened. Since you cannot undo the past no matter how hard you try, wipe the slate clean and go on to what's next. And remember, as the saying goes, "New beginnings can only come from old endings."

The choices we make truly do make us. With each one, we change—for the better or the worse. Perhaps the wisest words I have ever read about choices were written by Portia Nelson in a piece entitled "Autobiography in Five Short Chapters":

Chapter 1: I walk down the street. There is a deep hole in the sidewalk. I fall in. I am lost—I am helpless. It isn't my fault. It takes forever to find a way out.

Chapter 2: I walk down the same street. There is a deep hole in the sidewalk. I pretend I don't see it. I fall in again. I can't believe I am in the same place, but it isn't my fault. It still takes a long time to get out.

Chapter 3: I walk down the same street. There is a deep hole in the sidewalk. I see it is there. I still fall in . . . it's a habit. My eyes are open. I know where I am. It is my fault. I get out immediately.

Chapter 4: I walk down the same street. There is a deep hole in the sidewalk. I walk around it.

Chapter 5: I walk down another street.

To be a successful leader, you need to know what you stand for and what you will stand up to. The key choices you make regarding how you will conduct yourself and lead others not only indicate what kind of leader you are, they determine what kind of leader you will become. Choose wisely.

The Choices You Make, Make You

APPLICATION EXERCISES

1. What major choices have changed your life? Each of us has made choices that set the course of our lives and change who we are. Spend some time in reflection and write down the major choices you have made. For each choice, write how it changed your circumstances *and* how it changed you as a person. If your list includes negative choices or missed opportunities, you may need to work through the emotions that come from them and then move on.

2. What key choices have you made (or will you make) to guide your leadership? In the chapter I describe the three major choices I made regarding my leadership:

> *Choice #1:* My standards for myself will be higher than what others might set for me.
>
> *Choice #2:* Helping people is more important than making them happy.
>
> *Choice #3:* My focus will be on the present.

What choices will you make? Spend some time writing them out (choose no more than five).

3. Are you prepared to make difficult choices? What enables leaders to make the right choices? And how do they decide? I believe the best way is to prepare themselves by working through many of them ahead of time. Look at the key choices you wrote down for exercise 2. For each one, write down the implications that will come as a result of those key choices (as I did). Being prepared is half the battle.

MENTORING MOMENT

When it comes to choices, there are two ways in which you can help the people you are mentoring. First, assess how much ownership they take for the decisions they make. If someone has a tendency to blame others or possesses a victim's mind-set, you need to point it out. People cannot reach their potential as leaders if they don't take complete responsibility for themselves and their actions. Second, help them process through what choices they should make to become better leaders. Don't try to tell them what to choose. Instead, ask questions to get them to think it through so that they can discover the right choices and personally own them.

21

INFLUENCE SHOULD BE
LOANED BUT NEVER GIVEN

I've met people who think I make too big a deal about leadership. When I say, "Everything rises and falls on leadership," they are quick to start looking for exceptions. But I have yet to find one. I believe the proverb is true: "When good people run things, everyone is glad, but when the ruler is bad, everyone groans."[1]

For more than thirty years, I've worked to teach other people how to be better leaders. That means trying to help them become more influential. After all, leadership is influence, nothing more, nothing less. For example, several years ago, my friend Jim Dornan and I wrote a book entitled *Becoming a Person of Influence*. We created it to help people increase their influence potential. And for years I have given a lecture called "The Five Levels of Leadership." I've delivered it hundreds of times. Why? Because it helps people to understand how influence works and shows them how to expand their influence with others.

Leadership really does make a difference. One person with a lot of influence can make a huge positive impact on society. That's why Charles, Count Talleyrand, remarked, "I am more afraid of an army of one hundred sheep led by a lion than an army of one hundred lions led by a sheep." If you want to make an impact, then work on your influence. If you want to add value to others, help them work on theirs. That's why I have identified my life purpose as adding value to leaders (influencers) who multiply value to others.

THE VALUE OF INFLUENCE

I believe the pursuit of influence isn't meant to be selfish or negative. Influence has a purpose greater than that of bettering the life of the influencer. Boiled down to its essence, influence has value for three purposes:

1. Influence Exists to Speak Up for Those Who Don't Have Influence

One of the greatest responsibilities of leaders is to speak up for those who don't have influence. For many generations in America, people of African descent needed a voice to be heard on their behalf. In the twentieth century, Martin Luther King Jr. provided that voice. He was a person of both compassion and action who spoke for the suffering and poor and showed everyone a way toward change and healing. Any leader who does not lift up the lives of other people is not fulfilling the highest calling of being a leader.

2. Influence Exists to Speak to Those Who Do Have Influence

Another value of leadership is the ability to influence the influential. It is often difficult for anyone but a leader to get the ear of another leader. Often I have the privilege of sitting down with leaders in the corporate, government, religious, and educational communities. Why am I able to do it? Because I have worked hard to help people for forty years and have been recognized as a leader. I don't take the privilege for granted, and I try to use it to make a difference.

3. Influence Exists to be Passed On to Others

There are certain things that only leaders can do. One of them is developing other leaders. It takes a leader to raise up another leader. People of influence often have the opportunity of singling out potential leaders and helping them build a solid foundation upon which to develop their leadership. That is what this chapter is about.

Help Along the Way

When leaders are early in their journey, they don't possess much influence of their own. I think it's natural for young talented leaders to work hard and get less credit and recognition than they deserve for their efforts, and it's natural for older established leaders to receive more credit than they deserve for theirs. Young leaders aren't that bad, and old leaders aren't that good!

I feel that I was very fortunate because established leaders helped me along by using their influence to assist me when I was trying to make my way as a young leader. To them I will be forever grateful. People like Les Parrott, a successful author, opened the door for me to get my first book published. Carl George and the Charles Fuller Institute gave me a national platform as a speaker that greatly multiplied my influence as a leader. Ron Land, a former executive at Thomas Nelson, leveraged his influence to introduce me to important distribution channels for my books. And Bill Bright, the founder of Campus Crusade, put his arm around me and told thousands of people, "John is a leader you can trust." He gave me credibility it would have taken me a decade to earn.

> *"I am more afraid of an army of one hundred sheep led by a lion than an army of one hundred lions led by a sheep."*
> *—Count Talleyrand*

The list could go on and on. But this I know. I stand today on the shoulders of dozens of leaders who loaned me their influence at critical times of my life. I will be forever indebted and grateful to them.

Giving Away My Influence

I can remember when my influence as a leader began to turn. Suddenly it seemed that I didn't need the influence of others to open doors for me and give me credibility. I was developing my own reputation as a leader. It felt good to be able to stand on my own two feet and to add value to more people.

Around that same time, something else that I hadn't expected began to occur. People started asking me to extend my influence for them. Because my motivation as a leader was to help people, I gladly gave my influence to whoever asked for it—with no strings attached. Bad decision. I soon discovered that people were taking advantage of me. Here's what I mean:

They Failed to Establish Their Own Leadership Using My Influence

As a young leader, whenever I had received a more experienced leader's influence, I saw it as an opportunity to establish myself. The leader had opened the door; it was my job to make the most of it. I worked very hard to gain credibility for myself and prove myself.

That wasn't always the case with people to whom I gave my influence. Many enjoyed receiving an opportunity that my influence provided, but didn't *do* anything with it. They didn't establish themselves; instead they assumed that they would always have my influence to fall back on. When my influence wore off and they were "low," they would come back to me and ask for more. They would request my public support one more time. They would ask me to open doors for them again. They would ask me to enlist more of my followers to help them again.

I had used my influence to give them enough time to build their own credibility with people. But they didn't. And because I had given them my influence without conditions or expectations, I was spending a lot of time affirming them to others and propping them up. If leaders can't eventually lead on their own, then they are of little value to the organization.

They Took My Influence for Granted

When people expect you to continually bail them out and keep using your influence to establish their leadership position, it's one more short step for them to start taking your influence for granted. That's what often happened with me. A weak leader's lack of effort and experience often developed into an attitude issue. They got used to my intervention when they got in trouble and began to expect it. While I was waiting for them to step up, they were waiting for me to step in. They hoped I would carry more and more of their load. It's much easier to shine when someone else is carrying your weight. Some even began asking why I didn't come to their rescue more quickly when they needed help.

They Were Unable to Build the Organization by Passing on Influence to Others

As I've already mentioned, one of the most compelling reasons to develop influence is so that you can pass it on to others. People who have no influence of their own cannot pass on influence to others. You cannot give what you do not have. Why is that important? The way to grow an organization is to develop leaders. If the people you lead can't do that, then you have a built-in lid that will limit your organization. People who continually borrowed influence from me couldn't loan it to others. Therefore there was never any development or multiplication of leaders under their care.

LET'S CALL THIS A LOAN

When I was giving my influence to others unconditionally, the good news was that my motives were right. The bad news was that I was showing poor discernment as a leader. Giving influence to people who can't or won't use it appropriately is a waste of a leader's time, effort, and resources. It's like giving gold to someone who is going to bury it in their backyard and forget about it.

What I finally realized was that influence should never be given to others; it should only be loaned! It's like an investment, and you should expect a return. Just like a financial investment, when there isn't a good return, you should invest elsewhere. Only a fool sends good money after bad.

Now that I see things differently, I follow some guidelines that help me to loan my influence. Perhaps they will help you as others ask you to use your influence for them.

Not Everyone Will Receive the Loan of My Influence

Just as a bank will qualify a loan before money exchanges hands, so do I with my influence. Before I give people my endorsement and work to open doors for them, I want to know who they are. I want to understand their character. I want to know why they want the loan. I want to see that they have a game plan for using the "investment." And I want to know how they intend to pay it back with results.

Those Who Receive the Loan of My Influence Will Be Accountable

Before when I gave people my influence, I made assumptions about how they were using it and whether they would follow through on their plans. I don't do that anymore. I now recognize that it is my business as the influencer to know their business and make sure my investment is wise. To do that, I periodically check up on them to make sure the "transaction" was a wise one and that it is paying off.

I Expect a Good Return on My Loan

When I use my influence to benefit people, I expect them to become better leaders as a result. I want to *see* their growth accelerate. I want to *know* their influence has increased. My time and resources are limited. I'm sixty years old. I want every leadership investment I make to count. If they're not improving as a result—and using their influence to raise up other leaders themselves—then I reserve the right to stop investing and help someone else.

~

Today when I invest my influence in a potential leader, I do so very carefully. I take a long look at the person. I ask a lot of questions. And I make certain that the conditions are clear—that it's a loan, not a gift. And then, if everything looks right, I loan my influence to them, gladly and graciously. Why? Because it is an investment I want to make. Potential leaders have great potential to make an impact in the future with their influence.

Recently I wrote something that expresses exactly how I feel about this issue. I call it "My Loan Contract for Potential Leaders":

I can give you a position of leadership.
You must earn permission to lead.
I can give you an opportunity to lead.
You must make the best of that opportunity.

I can set you up as a leader with potential.
You must stay up by fulfilling your potential.
I can get people to follow you today.
You must get people to follow you tomorrow.
My influence to you is a loan, not a gift.
Express gratitude, and use it wisely.
Give me a return on my investment.
Give others a return on my investment.
Give yourself a return on my investment.

One of the people I am investing in and loaning my influence to is Chris Hodges, a wonderful leader and friend who lives in Birmingham, Alabama. Chris leads with a quiet, humble strength. Recently I received a note from him that said,

> John, you have added value to me by being valuable yourself. You couldn't add value to me unless you were valuable. You have allowed me to borrow your influence, name, relationships, and wisdom. I have met people I never would have met, trained leaders I never would have trained, and reached a level of leadership I could never have attained on my own, without your influence. Thanks!

The things I've given Chris that he described in that note were not accidental. I was very intentional in my desire to give him access to people and resources that he had not yet earned with his own influence, to give him a following he had not yet gathered using his own leadership, and to help him experience a degree of success that he had not yet achieved on his own.

I am so glad to help him. I have seen the influence Chris already had increase dramatically in recent years. And he is multiplying that influence by developing many leaders on his own. He maximizes everything he receives, and he never comes back looking for me to give him more. When he comes back, it is to try to give to me. Chris has a very bright future ahead of him!

I don't know where you are when it comes to your interaction with others in this area. If you currently have influence and are giving it to others indiscriminately, then I strongly encourage you to start *loaning* it instead.

What if you don't have much influence of your own? If that's the case, you have a different problem. You need to make yourself a candidate for influence—whether you earn it from your people or receive a loan of it from another more experienced leader. Either way, you can do that by cultivating the following characteristics:

- Insight: what you know
- Ability: what you do
- Character: who you are
- Passion: what you feel
- Success: what you achieve
- Intuition: what you sense
- Confidence: how secure you make others feel
- Charisma: how you connect

If you embody those characteristics, your influence will increase. Others will admire you, be attracted to you, and naturally begin to follow you. Once you have a following, you will be able to begin helping others. And when you do, remember: influence should be loaned, but never given.

INFLUENCE SHOULD BE LOANED
BUT NEVER GIVEN

APPLICATION EXERCISES

1. Are there people you need to speak up for? The movie *Amazing Grace* was the story of William Wilberforce, a British member of Parliament in the eighteenth century who spent his entire career working to get Great Britain to abolish slavery. Are there people who need you to stand up and speak for them? How can you use your influence to help others who cannot otherwise help themselves?

2. What do you expect in return for your influence? If you have any influence at all, you can use it to help other leaders who have less influence. Are you doing that? Begin loaning it to others who will make good use of it. And be sure to express your expectations to them up front. You may want to try using my loan contract for potential leaders.

3. Do you need to increase your level of influence with others? If you don't have the influence you would like, try working on the eight things listed in the chapter:

- Insight: reflect daily so that evaluated experience makes you wiser
- Ability: learn about your craft daily and do it with excellence
- Character: hold yourself to the highest standard of integrity daily
- Passion: figure out what your main thing is and engage in it daily
- Success: maximize your time daily to achieve results
- Intuition: pay attention to the intangibles of leadership daily
- Confidence: know what you're doing and make others feel confident daily
- Charisma: focus on others and show them you care daily

If you work on these, you will increase your influence with others, and you will also make yourself a candidate for an influence loan from others.

Mentoring Moment

When you decided to start mentoring people, you probably expected some kind of return in productivity for the investment you made. If you have not spelled out those expectations, do so now. Explain how and why you expect the people you mentor to grow. Outline what kind of influence of their own you expect them to develop. Ask them to begin stepping up immediately.

22

FOR EVERYTHING YOU GAIN, YOU GIVE UP SOMETHING

What is the key to going to the next level as a leader? Put another way, what is the greatest obstacle you will face once you have begun achieving your goals and tasting success? I believe it is the ability to let go of what you have so that you can reach for something new. The greatest obstacle leaders face can be their own achievement. In other words, as Rick Warren says, "The greatest detriment to tomorrow's success is today's success."

In 1995, I faced one of the most difficult decisions of my life. I was twenty-six years into a highly successful career as a pastor. I was in as good a position as I could be. I was forty-eight years old and at the top of my game. The church I was leading, Skyline Wesleyan Church, was at

> *"The greatest detriment to tomorrow's success, is today's success."*
> *—Rick Warren*

that time the "flagship" church of the denomination. It had a national reputation and was highly influential. The church and I were highly respected. My reputation with the people was golden. I had spent more than a decade developing leaders, and the congregation was very solid. And it was in San Diego, California, one of the most beautiful cities in the country. It was ideal—both financially and professionally. I believe I could have settled in there and stayed until I retired. The only major obstacle that lay before me was the relocation of the church, which I believe we could have accomplished. (The leader who succeeded me has since accomplished it.)

I had only one problem. I wanted to go to the next level as a leader. I wanted to make a national and international impact. And I couldn't do it if I stayed there. I realized that the next stage of growth for me would require many difficult changes and much more time than I could give while leading the church. I understood that I needed to answer one critical question: am I willing to give up all that I have for a new level of growth?

WHAT IS THE NEXT LEVEL WORTH?

That's a question that every leader must ask him- or herself more than once in a successful career. In *Leading Without Power,* Max DePree writes, "By avoiding risk, we really risk what is most important in life—reaching toward growth, our potential and a true contribution to a common goal."

I started learning this lesson about trade-offs as a child. My father would often admonish me by saying, "Pay now—play later." In fact, he said it a lot because I was someone who loved to play and *never* wanted to pay! What he was trying to teach me was to do the difficult things first, and then enjoy myself. I learned from him that we all pay in life. Anything we get will exact a price from us. The question is, when will we pay? The longer we wait to pay, the greater the price. It is like interest that compounds. A successful life is a series of trade-offs. In my career, over and over I have traded security for opportunity. I've given up what many would consider an ideal position so that I could grow as a leader or make a bigger impact.

> *"By avoiding risk, we really risk what is most important in life—reaching toward growth, our potential and a true contribution to a common goal."*
> *—Max DePree*

I've found that the higher we go, the harder it is to make trade-offs. Why? We have so much more that we risk giving up. People often talk about the sacrifices they had to make in the beginning of their careers. But in truth, most people have very little to give up in the beginning. The only thing of value that they have is time. But as we climb higher, we have more, and we find it more difficult to let go of what we've worked for. That's why many climb partway up the mountain of their potential and then stop. They come to a place where they are unwilling to give up something in order to get the next thing. As a result, they stall—some forever.

As I debated the trade-offs of leaving the church to become a full-time writer, speaker, and developer of people, I sought advice from a few trusted mentors. One of them, author and consultant Fred Smith, passed on the following thoughts to me:

> Something in human nature tempts us to stay where we're comfortable. We try to find a plateau, a resting place, where we have comfortable stress and adequate finances. Where we have comfortable associations with people, without the intimidation of meeting new people and entering strange situations. Of course, all of us need to plateau for a time. We climb and then plateau for assimilation. But once we've assimilated what we've learned, we climb again. It's unfortunate when we've done our last climb. When we have made our last climb, we are old, whether forty or eighty.

That pushed me over the edge. I resigned. I would strive to go to a new level or fail trying!

WHAT WILL YOU TRADE?

Soon after I resigned, I did some reflecting on the price of growth, and I wrote a lesson called "Ten Trade-Offs Worth Making." I believe the lessons I learned that have served me well may also serve you.

1. Trade Affirmation for Accomplishment

I've already explained that when I began my career, I was a people pleaser. I wanted approval from my followers, admiration from my peers, and awards from my superiors. I was an affirmation junky. But accolades are like smoke that quickly fades away. Awards turn to rust. And financial rewards are quickly spent. I decided that I would prefer to actually get something *done* than to just make myself look good. That decision paved the way for most of the other trades I would make in life.

2. Trade Security for Significance

Success does not mean simply being busy. What you give your life to matters. The great leaders in history were great not because of what they owned or earned but because of what they gave their lives to accomplish. They made a difference!

I chose a career in which I expected to make a difference. But that did not exempt me from having to take risks to do things of greater significance. The same will be true for you, no matter what profession you have chosen.

3. Trade Financial Gain for Future Potential

One of life's ironies for me is that I was never motivated by money, yet Margaret and I ended up doing well financially. Why? Because I was always willing to put future potential ahead of financial gain.

The temptation is almost always to go for the cash. But this goes back to the idea of pay now, play later. If you are willing to sacrifice financially on the front end for the possibility of greater potential, you are almost always given greater chances for higher rewards—including financially.

4. Trade Immediate Pleasure for Personal Growth

If ever there was something our culture has a difficult time with, it is delayed gratification. If you look at the statistics on how much people are in debt and how little they put into savings, you can see that people are always seeking immediate pleasure.

When I was a kid, school bored me, and I couldn't wait to be done with it. I would have liked nothing better than to drop out, marry Margaret, my high school sweetheart, and play basketball. But because I wanted to have a career in leadership, I went to college, earned my degree, and waited until after graduation to marry Margaret. That was a *very long* four years.

Time after time, Margaret and I have put off or sacrificed pleasures, conveniences, or luxuries in order to pursue personal growth opportunities. We've never regretted it.

5. Trade Exploration for Focus

Some people like to dabble. The problem with dabbling is that you never really become great at anything. True, when you are young, you should try out new things—see where your strengths and interests lie. But the older you are, the more focused you should be. You can only go far if you specialize in something. If you study the lives of great men and women, you will find that they were very single-minded. Once you have found what you were created to do, stick with it.

6. Trade Quantity of Life for Quality of Life

I have to confess that I have a "more" mentality. If one is good, four is better. If somebody says he can hit a goal of twenty, I encourage him to reach for twenty-five. When I teach a one-hour leadership lesson on CD, I want to put so much content in it that the people who receive it will have to listen to it five times to get everything they can out of it.

Because of this natural inclination to do more, I've often had very little margin in my life. For years my calendar was booked solid, and I took very little time to relax. I remember asking my brother and his wife to come visit me, and Larry saying, "No, you're too busy. If we come, we won't ever see you."

I once read that the president of a large publishing company sought out a wise man to get his advice. After describing the chaos that was his life, he silently waited to hear something of value from the sage. The older man at first said nothing. He simply took a teapot and began pouring tea into a cup. And he kept pouring until the tea overflowed and began to cover the table.

"What are you doing?" the businessman exclaimed.

"Your life," responded the wise man, "is like a teacup, flowing over. There's no room for anything new. You need to pour out, not take more in."

It has been very difficult for me to change my mind-set from quantity to quality. Honestly, I'm still working on it. Having a heart attack in 1998 certainly made an impact on me in this area. So did having grandchildren. I now carve out more time for the really important things in my life. I suggest you do the same.

7. Trade Acceptable for Excellent

This one is so obvious that it almost goes without saying. People do not pay for average. They are not impressed by anything that is merely acceptable. Leaders cannot rise up on the wings of mediocrity. If something is worth doing, give it your best—or don't do it at all.

8. Trade Addition for Multiplication

When people make the shift from doer to leader, they greatly increase the impact that their lives can make. It is a significant jump because, as I assert in *The 17 Indisputable Laws of Teamwork*, one is too small a number to achieve greatness. However, there is another jump that is more difficult and has even greater significance—changing from adder to multiplier.

> **Leaders who gather followers add to what they can accomplish. Leaders who develop leaders multiply their ability.**

Leaders who gather followers *add* to what they can accomplish. Leaders who develop leaders *multiply* their ability. How is that? For every leader they develop or attract, they gain not only that individual's horsepower but the horsepower of all the people that person leads. It has an incredible multiplying effect. Every great leader, regardless of where or when they led, was a leader of leaders. To go to the highest level of leadership, you must learn to be a multiplier.

9. Trade the First Half for the Second Half

In his book *Halftime*, Bob Buford says that most people who are successful in the first half of their life try to do the second half of their life in the same way. What he's really saying is that they reach a plateau and they are unwilling to trade what they have for a new way of doing things because it's much easier to stick with what's familiar.

If you are in the second half of life, you have probably spent much of your time paying the price for success. Don't waste it. Be willing to trade it for significance. Do things that will live on after you are gone. If you are in the first half, keep paying the price so that you have something to offer in your second half.

10. Trade Your Work for God for a Walk with God

As someone who has worked in ministry for many years, I understand the deep satisfaction of doing work that is for God. However, I also understand the trap of constantly doing *for* God without continually connecting *with* God.

If you are not a person of faith, then this may not make sense to you. However, if faith is a part of your life, remember that no matter how much value your work has, it cannot compare with a relationship with your creator.

ARE YOU WILLING TO GIVE UP TO GO UP?

To be an excellent leader, I think you have to learn to travel light. You must learn to off-load before trying to reload. You have to let go of one thing in order to grasp a new one. People naturally resist that. We want to stay in our comfort zone and hold onto what's familiar. Sometimes circumstances force us to give up something and we have the chance to gain something new. But more often than not, if we want to make positive trades, we have to maintain the right attitude and be willing to give up some things.

> *To be an excellent leader, I think you have to learn to travel light. You must learn to off-load before trying to reload.*

During the Civil War, President Abraham Lincoln was given a request for five hundred thousand additional recruits to fight in the army. Political advisors strongly recommended he turn it down since they thought honoring the request would prevent his reelection. But Lincoln's decision was firm.

"It is not necessary for me to be reelected," he said, "but it is necessary for the soldiers at the front to be reinforced by five hundred thousand men and I shall call for them. If I go down under the act, I will go down with my colors flying."

Lincoln is one of our greatest presidents because he was willing to give up everything—except final responsibility. That is the kind of attitude leaders need to have. Every new level of growth we hope to experience as leaders calls for a new level of change. You cannot have one without the other. If you want to be a better leader, get ready to make some trades.

As I've mentioned, I turned sixty in February of 2007. A few months before my birthday, I took the time to memorize the following prayer, because I wanted to pray it in the presence of my family and friends on my birthday. It says:

Lord, as I grow older, I think I want to be known as . . .
Thoughtful, rather than gifted,
Loving, versus quick or bright,
Gentle, over being powerful,
A listener, more than a great communicator,
Available, rather than a hard worker,
Sacrificial, instead of successful,
Reliable, not famous,
Content, more than driven,
Self-controlled, rather than exciting,
Generous, instead of rich, and
Compassionate, more than competent,
I want to be a foot-washer.

I'm still striving to become that person. I'm still making trades.

Now more than ever I am aware that a person's significant birthdays can either mark the passage of time, or they can mark changes they've made in their lives to reach their potential and become the person they were created to be. With each passing year, I want to make good choices that make me a better person, help me become a better leader, and make a positive impact on others. That requires a willingness to keep making trades, because for everything you gain, you have to give up something.

To see a video clip of John Maxwell teaching more on this leadership principle and to access additional helpful tools and information, visit www.johnmaxwell.com/leadershipgold.

For Everything You Gain, You Give Up Something

APPLICATION EXERCISES

1. What trades have you made? Take a look at the ten trades listed in the chapter:

1. Affirmation for Accomplishment
2. Security for Significance
3. Financial Gain for Future Potential
4. Immediate Pleasure for Personal Growth
5. Exploration for Focus
6. Quantity of Life for Quality of Life
7. Acceptable for Excellent
8. Addition for Multiplication
9. The First Half for the Second Half
10. Your Work for God for a Walk with God

Which of them would you say you have made in the past? (If you cannot cite a *specific* example, you have not made the trade.) Was the trade worth it? Why?

2. What additional trades do you need to make? The ten items above constitute my list. What additional trades need to be put on your list? Spend some hours reflecting on other trades you have already made, both positive and negative. Then create your own list of trades that you believe will benefit you in the future.

3. What will you trade for the betterment of your people? Max DePree said, "The first responsibility of a leader is to define reality. The last is to say thank you. In between, the leader is a servant." What are you willing to give up for the benefit of your people and organization? Will you forgo perks and privileges? Will you take less compensation? Will you give away the credit and take the blame?

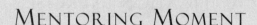

MENTORING MOMENT

Now that they are acquainted with the concept of trading up, ask the people you're mentoring what they are hoping to trade up to. They may respond by naming their ultimate personal goal, but ask them to focus on what would constitute the next phase in the journey. Talk to them about what they currently possess worth trading, and what they might have to give up to achieve the next thing. One of the greatest values of mentors is the ability to see ahead what others cannot see and to help them navigate a course to their destination.

23

THOSE WHO START THE JOURNEY WITH YOU SELDOM FINISH WITH YOU

Whenever I walk through Chicago's O'Hare Airport and pass a particular bank of pay phones, my mind races back to an incident that happened there in 1980. By then I had been leading for eleven years. In the first several years of my leadership, the organization I led was so small that Margaret and I did everything. But by this time, I had begun to gather and build a team. That was something I had longed and planned for. From the time I began my career, I had envisioned what my team would be like. We would be of one mind and spirit. We would do great things. We would stay together forever.

One of the first team members that I selected was my assistant, "Sue." She was a close friend of Margaret's and mine, and she was extremely capable. The first few years were just as I hoped and dreamed. Sue did a great job for me, and Margaret and I did many things together with Sue and her husband. A job doesn't feel like work when you're doing it with good people you love.

When an opportunity for advancement in my career came, I naturally wanted Sue to come with me. This would entail moving to another city, but she and her husband agreed that they wanted to keep working alongside us. Margaret and I were elated. Before long, the four of us traveled together to what would be our new city and went house hunting together. Everything was moving along, we were making plans, and we were excited about what the future held.

A couple of weeks later, while I was traveling, I called Sue back at the office from the Chicago airport. Usually she was very cheery. That wasn't the case this day. We talked business for a few minutes, but she soon interrupted the conversation.

"John, I have to tell you something," she blurted. "We're not moving. My husband and I have decided to stay where we are."

I was numb. *What happened?* I thought as I found my way to my gate. It was obvious that our paths would soon part. I was very sad and disappointed. As I boarded the plane, a leadership truth became clear in my mind despite the pain I was feeling: those who start the journey with you seldom finish it with you.

FEW GO THE DISTANCE

This lesson has probably been the most emotional one for me to write about. I'm a highly relational person. I enjoy people, and I especially enjoy doing things together as a team. I've led a lot of teams and studied teamwork for more than forty years. In 2001, I wrote a book called *The 17 Indisputable Laws of Teamwork*. In that book I wrote about the importance of my team and what it does for me:

My team is my joy. I would do anything for the people on my team because they do everything for me:

My team makes me better than I am.
My team multiplies my value to others.
My team enables me to do what I do best.
My team gives me more time.
My team represents me where I cannot go.
My team provides community for our enjoyment.
My team fulfills the desires of my heart.

At that time, I listed the twelve key players on my team who comprised my inner circle. Today only six remain on my team. It is a sad truth that those closest to you now may not always be those closest to you.

All Aboard!

In my early years of leadership, I assumed that everyone on my team would take the journey with me, and I thought it was my responsibility to make sure that they did. If the organization was like a train going down a track, then I was the engineer and the conductor. I drove the train and made sure everyone was on board. If we stopped for a rest break, at the time of departure I would call out, "All aboard." If my people did not come, I would go get them. If they did not want to get back on board, I would

Anytime you ignore reality for the sake of the relationship, you will have problems.

carry them on, take them to their seat, and serve them a snack. Whatever it took, I was determined to get them on board with me for the journey.

I've learned a lot since then. It took me a few years, but I finally discovered that . . .

Not Everyone Will Take the Journey with You

Being on a team is a choice. I found out that some of the people I wanted on my team didn't want to be on it. Sometimes it was a passion issue. My passion was not everyone's, and what motivated me didn't always motivate others. Some people didn't like the makeup of my team. Others simply didn't like me. And sometimes people had a different calling. Had I learned this earlier, my recruitment of potential team members would have been much easier.

Not Everyone Should Take the Journey with You

Just because you like people doesn't mean you need to have them on your team. Too often I would try to drag friends onto "my train." We enjoyed each other and thought we should work together. But often they didn't have the right skills or experience to contribute to the team. When I put them on the team anyway, it was always a mistake. Anytime you ignore reality for the sake of the relationship, you will have problems.

Not Everyone Can *Take the Journey with You*

Just because people were right for the team in the beginning of the journey doesn't mean they will always have the capacity to take the whole trip. Some simply do not possess the potential to grow as the vision and team do.

This realization was especially difficult for me. When memories of the early days of working with someone are wonderful, it becomes very difficult to face when those days are gone and will never return. But the reality is that as an organization grows, it sometimes outgrows some team members. It's like a train that starts out with an underpowered locomotive. When there are few cars to be pulled, the small amount of horsepower is not a problem. But as you add more and more cars to the train and try to climb uphill, sometimes people who had been pulling weight for the team become a weight to be pulled by the leader. And no matter how much time and effort you give to helping them improve, they are working at their full capacity and will never get any better.

One of the toughest decisions for leaders comes when they find themselves in such a situation with an employee. Do you continue to carry the person? If you do, it will diminish your leadership effectiveness and eventually exhaust you. Do you expect the team to keep carrying him? That will harm the team's momentum and morale. Do you fire him?

Ideally, you would try to find a place in the organization that matches his horsepower, where he can work to his potential. Some people will accept such a move gladly, just to be a part of the organization. Others can't or won't accept a demotion. If that is the case, all you can do is try to bless them as they leave.

Make no mistake, to some degree, you choose who you lose. If you keep and reward uncommitted or unproductive people, eventually your team will be comprised of uncommitted and unproductive people. What gets rewarded is what gets done. All organizations have turnover. People come and people go. The question is not, are people leaving? The question is, who is leaving? If the people joining your team have high potential and those leaving have limited potential, the team's future is bright. If those who are coming on board are limited and those who are leaving are gifted, your future is dim.

I have finally come to accept that it's okay for people to leave. People have left my teams for various reasons. I outgrew some. Some outgrew me. A few changed and wanted to go in a new direction. Some refused to change and the train had to leave them behind. This is one of the hard truths of leadership. Times change and people

> *The question is not, are people leaving? The question is, who is leaving?*

have to learn to move on. For some that can be very hard. However, if you call someone and get an answering machine message that says, "I am not available right now, but I thank you for caring enough to call. I am making some changes in my life. Please leave a message after the beep. If I don't return your call, you are one of the changes,"[1] you'll know that the individual succeeded.

GAINING PERSPECTIVE

It has not been fun leaving some people behind on the journey. I miss many of them. I hope some of them miss me too. But that's how leadership works. The best you can hope to do is be prepared as people leave and to maintain the right perspective on it. I hope some of my mistakes will help you. Here are four that I made and had to correct.

1. I Waited for People I Shouldn't Have Waited For

It is true that if you travel alone, you can rise up early. If you travel with others, you must wait on them. For some people, I simply waited too long. I held back and waited, but they never got back on board. Whenever I did that, the result was that the organization lost momentum, the sharpest members of my team became frustrated, and I lost credibility with people for not dealing with the situation more quickly. In desiring to do the right thing for an individual, I was doing the wrong thing for the organization.

2. I Felt Guilty When I Lost a Key Player

When I first started leading, whenever I lost a member of my team, I thought that it was a reflection on my leadership abilities. Sometimes it was. (If a leader keeps losing his best people, usually there is a problem with the leader.) But good leaders often identify and develop a lot of good people, and some of them eventually will leave the organization.

Early on in my career, I tried very hard to keep my best people—too hard, in fact. Many times I would offer big incentives to hold on to them. Most of the time when I did that, it was not the right decision. I had to learn that it is better to bless people as they go than it is to beg them to stay. You cannot effectively lead people who would rather not be on your team.

3. I Believed Important Players on My Team Couldn't Be Replaced

Anytime key people told me they were leaving the team, my first question would be, "Who can replace this person?" Too often I thought the answer was, "No one." I have since learned the fallacy of that thinking. There are good people everywhere, and they want to work for good leaders. The more you develop yourself as a leader and invest in people, the greater the pool of people to choose from.

This change in mind-set from scarcity to abundance has made a huge difference in the way I lead. For years I looked for good people to replace key players only after I received a resignation. Now I ask the question before there is a vacancy. That may seem callous, but when you are the point leader of an organization, the buck stops with you. You *must* be prepared for any situation because the team and organization rely on you for their success. For that reason, I try to have a substitute in mind for any key players on my team. That way, if someone leaves or a change occurs, I don't panic—and the team doesn't suffer.

4. I Had to Learn to Appreciate Those Who Were with Me for Only a Brief Time

The leadership journey is long, and there are seasons when a special person is needed to help a leader make the journey successfully. These highly skilled people often travel with a leader for only that season, and then they move on.

Many people have played that role in my life. They have come alongside me for a time and helped me navigate a certain passage in life. I no longer try to keep them with me. I recognize that some of them need to play this role with other leaders. Or they move on to a new season of their own. To them I am simply grateful. I recognize that getting to the next level would not have been possible without them.

≈

In the end, what I have discovered is that leaders cannot think of themselves as the owners of their teams—even if they happen to be the owner of the organization they lead. Good leaders understand that they are stewards. They must find the best people they can, giving them the opportunity to join in the journey developing them, and encouraging them to reach their potential. But they must hold on to people lightly. Those who start with you seldom finish with you.

The good news is that some will stay. For the few who continue on the journey with me, I am grateful. Each of them has given up something special so that together we could do something even more special together. Since they are so few, they are all the more precious to me. If you are still taking the journey with some of the people who began with you, celebrate, love them, reward them, and keep enjoying the journey.

APPLICATION EXERCISES

1. What is your reaction to people's leaving the team? How you respond when people leave can tell you a lot about your leadership. Do you take it personally? If so, you are perhaps leading out of insecurity. Do you panic? If so, you don't spend enough time looking for potential new leaders. Are you indifferent? If so, then you probably don't have enough of a relational connection with your people. Take some time to examine your response and see what it says about your leadership.

2. Have you been waiting too long for people to go to the next level? When everyone on the team believes that certain team members are holding the team back, it reduces the organization's momentum, hurts team chemistry, and undermines your leadership credibility. As the leader, you must deal with such people. If you don't, you will hurt the organization and your leadership. Determine what kind of issue you're dealing with. If it is . . .

- *Opportunity*, give them what they need to go to the next level.
- *Fit*, put them somewhere else that matches their strengths.
- *Potential*, find out if they have the *ability* to improve.
- *Attitude*, find out if they *want* to go to the next level.

If the issue is opportunity or fit, they may very well rise to the occasion. If it is potential, they may be able to function well at a lower level. If it is attitude, they must change or go.

3. Where are the next key players coming from? If you are not already looking for potential team members, begin today. Think about who in your organization might be able to step up in their area or step in from another department or position. Stay in contact with friends and colleagues who might be able to work with you or who might know others who could. You can even look for sharp people among your competitors. Keep your eyes open. Everyone you meet is a potential team member.

MENTORING MOMENT

Assist the people you are mentoring in identifying people who may be holding their team back. Help them to determine whether the issue is opportunity, fit, potential, or attitude. Be their coach and cheerleader as they work to address the issue.

24

FEW LEADERS ARE
SUCCESSFUL UNLESS A LOT OF
PEOPLE WANT THEM TO BE

In 1998, Jeffrey Katzenberg and Dreamworks SKG produced an animated feature film called *The Prince of Egypt*. The movie was about Moses, who grew up in Egypt as a member of Pharaoh's household and eventually guided the children of Israel out of Egyptian bondage. As the movie was being made, the producers invited a few religious leaders to consult with them about it. I had the privilege of being one of those leaders. The experience was very enlightening to me as I was able to observe some of what happened behind the scenes during the making of that film.

As the opening date for the film approached, Margaret and I were delighted to receive an invitation to attend the premiere. What an exciting night it was! The evening was filled with laughter and words of congratulations. Yes, there was a red carpet, camera crews, media, interviews, and movie stars. And yes, Margaret and I walked on the red carpet and waved to the crowd—who ignored us.

When we were inside the theater and the movie began, I noticed how focused everyone was. Certainly a few of the attendees had seen the completed film, but most of them, like us, were seeing it for the first time. And they all had one question on their minds: "How did the movie turn out?"

As we watched, the people responded positively to seemingly insignificant things to which a normal audience wouldn't. Why? Because they were involved in the details. It was a unique experience, and Margaret and I enjoyed the movie.

When it was over, the crowd applauded enthusiastically, and I quickly stood up to leave. Anyone who goes to an event with me knows that I like to exit early. Margaret quickly pulled me back down into my seat; nobody else in the theater had moved. Amazingly, excitement mounted as the credits began to roll. There were cheers as name after name rolled by, and the movie's stars were the main cheerleaders as the many support people were recognized for their vital part in the success of the movie.

Without a lot of people working together, there would be no successful leaders.

To the people in that theater, the credits were not just a bunch of random names. They were the names of individual people they knew and cared about who had made specific contributions to *The Prince of Egypt*. Without them, successful completion of the film would not have been possible. That night I left with the impression that everyone was valued because everyone was valuable. It takes a lot of people to create a success. That's why I say that few leaders are successful unless a lot of people want them to be.

NO SOLO LEADERS

I think sometimes there is a misconception that great leaders—especially the ones we read about from history—are able to accomplish big things regardless of what kind of help they receive from others. We believe individuals like Alexander the Great, Julius Caesar, Charlemagne, William the Conqueror, Louis XIV, Abraham Lincoln, and Winston Churchill would be great no matter what kind of support they got. But that simply isn't true. Without a lot of people working together, there would be no successful leaders.

Dan Sullivan and Catherine Nomura write in their book *The Laws of Lifetime Growth*,

Only a small percentage of people are continually successful over the long run. These outstanding few recognize that every success comes through the assistance of many other people—and they are continually grateful for this support. Conversely, many people whose success stops at some point are in that position because they have cut themselves off from everyone who has helped them. They view themselves as the sole source of their achievements. As they become more self-centered and isolated, they lose their creativity and ability to succeed. Continually acknowledge others' contributions, and you will automatically create room in your mind and in the world for much greater success. You will be motivated to achieve even more for those who have helped you. Focus on appreciating and thanking others, and the conditions will always grow to support your increasing success.[2]

If you want to be a successful leader, you will need the support of many people. And if you are wise, you will appreciate and acknowledge their contribution to your success.

HELP ALONG THE WAY

In the beginning years of my leadership journey I continually asked myself, "What can I accomplish?" My focus was too much on myself and what *I* could do. It didn't take long for me to discover that what I could accomplish on my own was quite insignificant. Self-made men don't make much. I quickly changed my question to be, "What can I accomplish with others?" I realized that success would be mine only if others helped me. As a leader, you will never get ahead until your people are behind you.

> *As a leader, you will never get ahead until your people are behind you.*

When I look back at all the people who have help me along over the years, I realize they fall into two main groups: mentors and supporters. The mentors taught me, guided me, and many times took me under their wing. I am so very grateful to them. Here's what's interesting about them:

Some Helped Me Who Never Knew Me

I cannot count the number of mentors I've had but have never met. Most of them have taught me through the books they've written or through what others have written about them and their ideas. They've reached across time to instruct me and their legacy lives on in me.

Some Who Knew Me Never Knew They Helped Me

Many people have modeled principles of leadership and success that I have been able to apply to my life. I watched them and learned many of the things that now add value to my life. When I get the opportunity, it is my joy to express my gratitude to these unintentional mentors.

Some Knew Me and Knew They Helped Me

These people have been intentional in their assistance. Some of them took under their wing a young leader who had no idea how much he didn't know. Others saw an emerging leader and guided him along. Some today continue helping me to sharpen my thinking and improve as a leader. Most of the good things that happen to me are a direct result of their commitment to add value to me.

❧

The mentors in my life have often reached down to me to draw me up to where they are. The supporters often take another role: they lift me up and make me better than I am on my own. As I think about all the different kinds of people who have taken and continue to take that role with me, I recognize that most of them fall into one of several categories. I'll list them because you may find it helpful for identifying the kinds of people who are also helping you:

- **Time Relievers**—people who save me time
- **Gift Complementers**—people who do things I am not gifted to do
- **Team Players**—people who add value to me and my team
- **Creative Thinkers**—people who solve problems and give me options
- **Door Closers**—people who complete assignments with excellence

- **People Developers**—people who develop and raise up other leaders and producers
- **Servant Leaders**—people who lead with the right attitude
- **Mind Stretchers**—people who expand my thinking and my spirit
- **Relational Networkers**—people who bring other people into my life who add value to me
- **Spiritual Mentors**—people who encourage me in my faith walk
- **Unconditional Lovers**—people who know my weaknesses, yet love me unconditionally

I am so grateful to these people. I respect, value, and appreciate them. I cannot be successful without them, and I let them know that on a daily basis. A Chinese proverb reads, "Behind an able man are always other able men [and women]." That has certainly been true in my life.

THE VISION DEPENDS ON OTHERS

I've had a lot of big dreams in my life. But God has never given me one that I could accomplish on my own. And because my dreams are always bigger than I am, I have only two choices: I can give up, or I can get help! I choose to seek help.

Most days when I'm not traveling, I work at my home office. But last week as I walked around our office complex, I was continually reminded of the fact that leaders are successful only when others want them to be.

In one office is a painting of my father, my brother, and me. Without question, many of the blessings in my life have come as a result of them. My father is one of the greatest influences in my life. He continues to be a hero to me. My brother, Larry, is one of my closest advisors and best friends.

> *"Behind an able man are always other able men and women."*
> —*Chinese proverb*

On the walls of the EQUIP offices, I see photographs of leaders from countries around the world who have partnered with the EQUIP team to train millions of leaders worldwide. The mission is impossible without them.

In the reception area of INJOY Stewardship Services (ISS) sits a Murano glass eagle, given to me by my publisher, Thomas Nelson, to commemorate the sale of ten million of my books. For many years their team has increased my value as a writer, and from many of our meetings have come great ideas that have lifted me to higher levels as an author. Where would I be without them?

In the hallways of ISS hang pictures of megachurches that have been built because of our expertise in raising finances. The many members of the ISS team have been my representatives to these churches and to many others as consultants and partners helping them succeed. None of that would have been accomplished without them.

I could go on and on. Each person plays a part in my success. Take them away, and what I can accomplish on my own becomes insignificant.

People appreciate working for someone who appreciates them.

What is my response as a leader when I understand this lesson? Gratitude, of course. I say thank you to the people who have lifted me on their shoulders. I know I am where I am because of them. The English word *thanks* comes from the same root word as *think*. Maybe if leaders were more "think-ful" about the contribution of others, they would be more "thankful" to them.

The truth is that success is compounded when others join our cause. Followers make leaders possible. Great followers make it possible for there to be great leaders. If you never learn that lesson as a leader, your effectiveness will never reach the highest level, and you will be forever recruiting members to a team with high turnover. People appreciate working for someone who appreciates them.

APPLICATION EXERCISES

1. *Who supports you?* What kinds of support people do you have working with you? Look at the list from the chapter:

- **Time Relievers**—people who save me time
- **Gift Complementors**—people who do things I am not gifted to do
- **Team Players**—people who add value to me and my team
- **Creative Thinkers**—people who solve problems and give me options
- **Door Closers**—people who complete assignments with excellence
- **People Developers**—people who develop and raise up other leaders and producers
- **Servant Leaders**—people who lead with the right attitude
- **Mind Stretchers**—people who expand my thinking and my spirit
- **Relational Networkers**—people who bring other people into my life who add value to me
- **Spiritual Mentors**—people who encourage me in my faith walk
- **Unconditional Lovers**—people who know my weaknesses, yet love me unconditionally

Think about how your people might fit into these categories. Are there other categories not listed that you value? If so, what are they? Finally, are there categories of support people with no one listed? How will you go about finding people to fill them?

2. *How do you say thank you?* An important part of being an effective leader is taking time to show appreciation for the people who are making you successful. How do you do that? Have you specifically told every person on your support list "thank you"? Have you told them what their contribution is and how much you value it? Do you reward them regularly? If you don't genuinely show your appreciation on a regular basis, you won't keep your people very long.

3. *Who are your mentors?* Who is currently guiding you and drawing you up to their level? If nobody is currently fulfilling that role in your life, find someone to do it. What about your mentors of the past? Have you thanked them? If not, take time this week to write notes of appreciation to let them know how grateful you are for how they have added value to you.

MENTORING MOMENT

Now is a good time to thank the people you are mentoring for the things they do to help you in your leadership. Spend some time reflecting about each person's contribution. Identify specifically what they do for you and how it helps. Then communicate that to them, both verbally and in writing. And reward them in some way too.

25

YOU ONLY GET ANSWERS TO THE QUESTIONS YOU ASK

Confidence can be defined as that uplifting, energizing, positive feeling that you possess—before you truly understand your situation. After graduating from college, I went into my first job with great confidence. I felt I was ready to take on the challenge of leading a small congregation. I thought it would be easy. But then I faced the reality of leading volunteers. It was so frustrating. I found out that I was not ready for the task. And I had no clue how to *get* ready.

I had so many questions, but my biggest problem was that my ego would not allow me to ask them. Instead, I pretended to know what I was doing. Believe me, that is not a great recipe for successful leadership! After a few months I became desperate. A Chinese proverb says, "He who asks is a fool for five minutes, but he who does not ask is a fool forever." I finally concluded that it would be better to *look* uninformed than to *be* uninformed. I decided to risk being a fool for five minutes and began asking questions.

> *Confidence can be defined as that uplifting, energizing, positive feeling that you possess—before you truly understand your situation.*

I'd like to be able to tell you that this instantly solved all my problems and turned everything around for me. But it didn't. Why? Initially my questions were not the right ones. But that didn't matter because I was also asking them of the wrong people! Fortunately, in time I discovered that if I persevered and kept asking questions, I would start figuring out the right questions to ask. And if I kept asking the right questions, it would eventually lead me to the right people. The process took me years. But here's the really good news: when you know the right questions and go to the right people with them, you will ultimately get the right answers!

> *"He who asks is a fool for five minutes, but he who does not ask is a fool forever."*
> —Chinese proverb

THE QUEST FOR THE RIGHT QUESTIONS

Not everyone discovers this secret. I read a hilarious story about three very competitive brothers who left home to make their fortunes, and each of them did very well. One day when they were all together, they started to brag about the gifts they had recently given to their elderly mother.

The first said, "I built Mom a big house."

The second said, "Well, I got her the best Mercedes they make along with her own driver."

"I've got you both beat," said the third. "You know how Mom enjoys the Bible, and you know she can't see very well. I sent her a brown parrot that can recite the entire Bible. It took twenty monks in a monastery twelve years to teach him. I had to contribute $100,000 to the order every year for ten years for them to train him, but it was worth it. Mom just has to name the chapter and verse, and the parrot will recite it."

Soon thereafter, each of the sons received a note from their mother. To the first son she wrote, "Milton, the house you built is so huge. I live in only one room, but I have to clean the whole house."

To the second son she wrote, "Marty, I am too old to go anywhere. I stay home all the time, so I never use the Mercedes. Besides, the driver is so rude!"

To the third son, her message was softer: "Dearest Melvin, you are the only son to have the good sense to know what your mother likes. The chicken was delicious."

Some people have to learn the importance of asking questions the hard way!

Asking questions often separates successful people from those who are unsuccessful. Why? Because you can only get answers to the questions you ask. No questions—no answers. As financier and presidential advisor Bernard Baruch said, "Millions saw the apple fall, but Newton was the one who asked why."

Some of the most stimulating moments of my life have come as the result of asking successful people questions and then listening to their responses. Early in my career, I made it a point to seek out leaders in my field who were the best in the country. I met with as many of them as I could and simply asked questions for thirty or more minutes. As they talked, I took notes. (My mother gave me good advice when she said, "Be a good listener. Your ears will never get you in trouble.") I can't explain how much the things I learned from them helped me in my career.

Even today, at age sixty, I still seek out successful leaders and ask them questions. I try to meet with some person I admire and respect at least half a dozen times a year. And before I do, I always spend a lot of time in preparation. Author Brian Tracy commented, "A major stimulant to creative thinking is focused questions. There is something about a well-worded question that often penetrates to the heart of the matter and triggers new ideas and insights." In general, the more thoughtful and precise the question, the better the answer. As speaker Anthony Robbins says, "Quality questions create a quality life. Successful people ask better questions and as a result, they get better answers."

THE FIRST PERSON TO ASK . . .

It's difficult for me to give you advice about whom you should talk to and what you should ask in order to grow and improve as a leader. It really depends on what work you do, where you are in your journey, and how you want to grow. However, I can tell you this: Before you run out and interview a bunch of leaders, you need to do something else first. You need to ask *yourself* a few questions. If you're not doing the right things to set the overall course for your life, then getting advice and answers from others will do little good. If you ask yourself the right questions and get on track as a leader, then what you should ask others will soon become clear.

Several years ago I wrote down ten questions that I felt I needed to periodically ask myself. I believe that answering these questions helped to get me on track, and they continue to keep me on track as a leader and help me grow as a person. I hope they will also add value to you.

"Quality questions create a quality life. Successful people ask better questions and as a result, they get better answers."
—*Anthony Robbins*

1. Am I Investing in Myself?—This Is a Personal Growth Question

I discussed this issue in great depth in the chapter "Keep Learning to Keep Leading," so I will only touch on it here. The reality is that leaders too often fail to fill themselves up enough to be able to give much to others. However, you cannot give what you do not have. Good leaders invest in themselves, and they do it not as an end unto itself but for the benefit of others. Learn more and you can lead better—and develop better leaders.

2. Am I Genuinely Interested in Others?—This Is a Motive Question

Whenever people tell me that they want to be leaders, I ask why. Sometimes their answers are about control or power. Other times I can tell that they are interested in the perks: a good parking place, the corner office, a better salary, a respected title, etc. Only rarely do I hear what I believe is the only right answer for wanting to be a leader: helping others.

Of all the ten questions I ask myself, this is the one I focus on most often. Why? Because I know what power can do to a person. It is very easy to move from being a serving leader to being a self-serving one. I say this because one of the qualities that all good leaders have is the ability to assess situations very quickly and come up with a game plan. They may not be smarter than others, but they are often quicker. How is that a problem?

Since leaders can evaluate quickly, they are often in a position to take care of their own needs and desires first—to set themselves up—before helping anyone else. That is *always* a temptation for a leader, and it is always wrong.

One of the best ways to guard against this temptation is to take a genuine interest in the people you lead. If you build relationships with them, learn about their hopes and dreams, and focus on helping them to reach their potential, you are much less likely to do things to violate the trust of your leadership position.

3. Am I Doing What I Love and Loving What I Do?—This Is a Passion Question

Often I am asked to give advice about living a successful life. There are a few universal principles that will enable a person to experience success. The one I always give first is, "You will never fulfill your destiny doing something you despise."

> *It is very easy to move from being a serving leader to being a self-serving one.*

Passion for what you do is at the core of your success and fulfillment. Passion will fuel you and give you energy when others around you grow tired. Passion will help you come up with answers when others cease to have creative ideas. Passion will strengthen your will when others drop out. Passion will give you courage to take a risk when others crave security. Passion will allow you to play while others work every day.

People have a tendency to get into ruts. I often ask myself, "Do I still love what I do or am I just doing what I do?" I want to make sure I'm still passionate because if I'm not, I know what can begin to happen. Leaders who continually do work that they dislike are in danger of not only failing to work with excellence, but they also put their integrity in jeopardy because they become tempted to compromise the wrong things or take shortcuts.

4. Am I Investing My Time with the Right People?—This Is a Relationship Question

Thirty years ago I heard Charles "Tremendous" Jones say, "Your life will be the same five years from now except for the people you meet and

the books you read." As a young man, I took him at his word. That's
when I began to seek out people whose lives
I admired. If I could get an appointment
with them, I would. If I couldn't, I'd buy
their teachings on tape or CD or attend their
conferences.

*Ask, "Do I still love
what I do or am I just
doing what I do?"*

The thesis of my book *Winning with People*
highlights the importance of the people in
our lives: "People can usually trace their successes and failures to the relationships in their lives." It's been my observation that

When I'm with the wrong people asking the wrong questions, I am
wasting my time.
When I'm with the right people asking the wrong questions, I am
wasting their time.
When I'm with the wrong people asking the right questions, I am
spending time.
When I'm with the right people asking the right questions, I am
investing my time.

I've said it before, but it bears repeating. Find the right people and ask
them the right questions if you want to keep growing as a leader.

5. Am I Staying in My Strength Zone?—This Is an Effectiveness Question

I've touched on this in the chapter "Get in the Zone and Stay There," so
you already know what I think in this area. Henry Ford remarked, "The
question, 'Who ought to be the boss?' is like asking, 'Who ought to be the
tenor in the quartet?' Obviously, the man who can sing tenor." Effective
executives build on strengths . . . their own strengths and the strengths of
their superiors, colleagues, and subordinates; and on their strengths in the
situation, that is, on what they can do. They do not build on weakness.
They do not start building on a foundation of things they cannot do. Know
what you do well and go with it!

6. Am I Taking Others to a Higher Level?—This Is a Mission Question

As I've stated, the question of a leader's effectiveness can only be answered by looking at the people who follow him. Are the people under his leadership getting better or getting worse? Are they going up or going down? Is their future getting brighter or darker?

As I travel to developing countries, I encourage leaders to ask themselves this question. Sadly, in many of these places things are getting better only for the leaders and a few of their favorites. But it is wrong for any leader to better himself while others suffer.

Every day I remind myself that my mission as a leader is to add value to others. That is the only reason that I should have the privilege of leading others. If others are going to a higher level, then I should continue leading. If the opposite is true, someone else should take my place.

7. Am I Taking Care of Today?—This Is a Success Question

The secret of your success is determined by your daily agenda. Successful people make right decisions early and then manage those decisions daily. I feel so strongly about this idea that I wrote an entire book on it called *Today Matters*. If I focus on today and do what it requires, then I am preparing for tomorrow. If I do not take care of today correctly, then tomorrow I will be fixing today's mistakes.

> *You will never change your life until you change something you do daily.*

People with vision want to change things to make for a better future. However, they can't actually *do* anything positive if they put all their focus on the future. When people ask me for advice about changing something in their lives, I tell them, "You will never change your life until you change something you do daily." Every day if you ask yourself, "Am I taking care of today?" you will be able to keep yourself on course, correct things quickly when you're off course, and create a better tomorrow.

8. Am I Taking Time to Think?—This Is a Strategic Leadership Question

The Achilles' heel of many leaders is too little thinking time. Leaders are naturally action-oriented people. They like to move themselves, others, and their organizations forward. They possess an innate restlessness. That often makes them resist the practice of setting aside enough thinking time so that they can lead most effectively.

Because I am highly energetic and active, I've had to discipline myself in this area and create systems that work for me. You may want to use them, too, in order to maximize your thinking time. My system looks like this:

- **I have a place to think my thoughts.** There is a comfortable chair in my office that I use only for creative and reflective thinking.
- **I have a way to shape my thoughts.** I have developed specific processes for developing and deepening any ideas I come up with.
- **I have a team to stretch my thoughts.** There are certain people in each area of my life who challenge me, add value to my ideas, and help me to improve my thinking.
- **I have a time to fly my thoughts.** Before going to the implementation phase, I test my ideas with others to make sure they will fly.
- **I have a place to land my thoughts.** Good thinking has limited value to leaders if it is never implemented. There are people within my organizations who are capable of taking any idea and making it a reality. I put my ideas in the hands of these people and then give them the resources and authority to make them happen.

This is probably enough information to help you engage in strategic thinking. However, if you want to sharpen your thinking and learn more about this subject, check out my book *Thinking for a Change.*

9. Am I Developing Other Leaders?—This Is a Legacy Question

As I told you in the beginning of this chapter, when I first started leading volunteers, I had trouble getting people to follow me. As I learned how to lead, I began to have followers. At first I thought that was quite an accomplishment. Only when I left my first organization and watched it fall apart did I realize my error. If you want an organization to be successful for any length of time, you can't just lead followers. You need to develop other leaders.

It took me a lot of time to learn how to develop leaders. And then it took even more time to actually do it. Now, after many years of focusing

my attention on leadership development, I understand that leading followers is fast and easy, and it has little return; leading leaders is slow and hard,
and it has great return. The price of developing leaders is very high—but
so is the return! I wouldn't lead any other way.

10. Am I Pleasing God?—This Is a Faith Question

This final question may not connect for you, but it is the most important one for me. I apologize if it offends you. But if I am going to have
integrity with you as I write, I must include it. One of the key questions of
my faith is, "What good will it be for a man if he gains the whole world, yet
forfeits his soul?"[1] My leadership and my life would fall short if what I was
doing didn't please God.

Some people see questions as a sign of ignorance. I see them as a sign
of engagement, curiosity, and the desire to improve—assuming that the
questions are thoughtful and the questioner doesn't keep asking the same
questions over and over again. If you're not asking, you're not advancing.
If you're not listening, you're not learning. (It's said that small people
monopolize the talking and big people monopolize the listening.) If you
don't ask questions, you won't get answers. And know this: if you are no
longer asking questions as a leader, then you might as well buy a rocking
chair, put it on your front porch, and call it a day, because you've already
retired!

You Only Get Answers to the Questions You Ask

APPLICATION EXERCISES

1. Is your ego getting in the way of your growth? How open are you to asking questions that may expose your ignorance or inexperience? Be honest: Are you afraid of looking stupid? Are you worried about what others will think of you? If you have been in leadership for a long time and have been reluctant to ask questions, it is going to be difficult to change. However, your choice is to look foolish for five minutes or be a fool forever. Start asking questions beginning today and work to manage your internal discomfort.

2. What questions do you need to ask yourself? You will never be an effective leader unless you hold yourself accountable for your actions and your growth. You cannot do those things without asking yourself some hard questions. Create your own questions or use ones in the chapter to make sure you are on track.

1. Am I investing in myself? (Personal Growth)
2. Am I genuinely interested in others? (Motive)
3. Am I doing what I love and loving what I do? (Passion)
4. Am I investing my time with the right people? (Relationships)
5. Am I staying in my strength zone? (Effectiveness)
6. Am I taking others to a higher level? (Mission)
7. Am I taking care of today? (Success)
8. Am I taking time to think? (Strategy)
9. Am I developing other leaders? (Legacy)
10. Am I pleasing God? (Faith)

3. Who can take your questions? Being willing to ask questions and risk looking foolish in front of others indicates a proper attitude toward learning. However, it does not constitute a plan for growth. Think about which people you would be able to learn from in order to grow and then try to get appointments to meet with them. Prior to a meeting, spend a minimum of two hours preparing for the interview and writing out your questions. (If the person has authored books, then read all of them before writing your questions. If he or she has produced lessons, listen to them first. For someone who has written or taught a lot, your preparation may take weeks.)

MENTORING MOMENT

Take this opportunity to address the issue of teachability with the people you're mentoring. How often are they asking questions? How open are they to taking advice—not only from you, but from their peers and the people who work for them? Discuss with them any issues you perceive in this area.

26

PEOPLE WILL SUMMARIZE YOUR LIFE IN ONE SENTENCE—PICK IT NOW

On December 18, 1998, I had a serious heart attack. That night as I lay on the floor waiting for an ambulance, I remember thinking two things: First, I was too young to die. Second, I had not completed some of the things I wanted to accomplish.

Thanks to excellent medical care and the prayers of many, I survived and am now in good health. But during my recovery, I thought a lot about life, death, and the impact I wanted to make before I died. As I considered what might have happened, I thought about who would have attended my memorial service. I wondered what people would say. And in an honest moment, I had to laugh as I realized that the size of my funeral attendance would be determined by the weather—and that thirty minutes after the service was done, people would be in some community building and the most important thing on their minds would be where to find the potato salad!

WHAT WILL I LEAVE BEHIND?

One of the most beneficial outcomes of my heart attack experience was that it motivated me to ask myself, "What will my legacy be?" A legacy is something we leave behind to the next generation. It can be possessions that we place in the hands of others. It can be principles we lived that carry on beyond our lives. It also can be people we have influenced whose lives are better as a result of knowing us.

Now that I am getting older and have begun to think more about my legacy, I ask leaders I admire about what they desire to leave behind after they die. A few years ago at a conference I hosted, I interviewed John Wooden, the legendary college basketball coach of the UCLA Bruins, who was ninety-two at that time. I asked him about his legacy and how he wanted to be remembered by those who knew him.

"I certainly don't want to be remembered for trophies and national championships," he said without hesitation. There was a rumble of surprise that ran through the audience. For a long time he paused, thinking. Finally he said, "I hope people will remember me as one who was kind and considerate of others." All of us were humbled by the simple wisdom he displayed, and we were reminded of the important difference between values and mere things. John Wooden achieved professional success beyond most people's wildest dreams, yet he wanted to be remembered for his treatment of others.

WHAT WILL *YOU* LEAVE BEHIND?

Someday you and I are going to die. And eventually our lives will be summarized in a single sentence. What do you want yours to be? Claire Booth Luce cleverly called this your "life sentence." If you are intentional about creating your legacy, people at your funeral won't have to wonder what your life sentence was.

Eleanor Roosevelt remarked, "Life is like a parachute jump, you've got to get it right the first time." Honestly, none of us gets it completely right. I think we all wish we could go back and make some changes in our lives. Yet we can choose to live our lives from today forward in such a way that we continue to make a positive impact on others after our death. We can create a legacy worth leaving. To accomplish this, I suggest that you do the following:

1. Choose Today the Legacy You Want to Leave Others
Legacies that are passed on to others can be intentional or unintentional. I've observed that most are *un*intentional. I received legacies from many

people who were not intentionally investing in me. For example, my Grandpa Maxwell was an example of determination and strong will. Grandma Roe was the first to share with me a great passion to travel. Mom gave me unconditional love. My fifth grade teacher, Mr. Horton, helped me see myself as a leader. Wayne McConnahey got me interested in sports. Each of them made a huge impact on my life that carries on to this day—my determination, love for travel, passion for leadership, and enjoyment of sports. However, I don't think any of them was consciously trying to pass these things on to me. They were simply being who they were, and I "caught" these qualities by being around them.

> *"The average man does not know what to do with his life, yet wants another one which will last forever."*
> —Anatole France

Nobel Prize–winning novelist Anatole France observed, "The average man does not know what to do with his life, yet wants another one which will last forever." Most people are not intentional about what legacy they want to create. They should be. Nobody will ever care about the legacy you leave as much as you do. If you don't take responsibility for it and see it through, then nobody else will.

Choose your legacy. Be intentional about it. That way you have the possibility of making a greater impact on a future generation. You can begin doing that today by defining your "life sentence." You won't figure it out all at once. If you're like me, you will need to refine it over time. I started thinking about my purpose in the late 1960s, and it has continued to evolve. Here is how my sentence has changed over the years along with my thinking:

I want to be a great pastor.
I want to be a great communicator.
I want to be a great writer.
I want to be a great leader.

As I grew and my horizons broadened, the sentence describing my purpose continued to change. Then there was a moment when I looked at those statements and realized that my desire to be an effective pastor, communicator, writer, and leader was really a desire to add value to people.

You'll notice that there has been a significant shift in my thinking, one that is critical to create a legacy intentionally. Now, instead of focusing on who I am to become, my focus is on other people. And I have since refined my life sentence even further. Now it's, **I want to add value to leaders who will multiply value to others.** When I die, I hope others will confirm that I have done exactly that.

Author and leadership expert John Kotter said to me once, "Most people don't lead their lives; they just accept them." Don't allow that statement to apply to you. Begin choosing the legacy you want to leave others. It may be just

> *"Most people don't lead their lives; they just accept them." —John Kotter*

the beginning of the process, but that's okay. You must start in order to finish.

2. Live Today the Legacy You Want to Leave

It's one thing to identify a legacy. It's another to pass it on. The greatest guarantee that you will leave the legacy you desire is how you live. In my book *Today Matters*, I point out that the secret of a person's success is determined by their daily agenda. I think it is also safe to say that the secret of your legacy is determined by your daily agenda. The sum of how you live each day becomes your legacy. Add up each action over the course of many years, and you can see your legacy beginning to take form.

In his book *Training for Power and Leadership*, Grenville Kleiser writes:

> Your life is like a book. The title page is your name, the preface your introductions to the world. The pages are a daily record of your efforts, trials, pleasures, discouragements, and achievements. Day by day your thoughts and acts are being inscribed in your book of life. Hour by hour, the record is being made that must stand for all time. Once the word "finis" must be written, let it then be said of your book that it is a record of noble purpose, generous service, and work well-done.

Most people don't get to choose when or how they're going to die. But they can decide how they're going to live. Sociologist Anthony Campolo tells about a study in which fifty people over the age of ninety-five were asked one question: "If you could live your life over again, what would you do differently?" The question was open-ended, and people's answers were varied. However, three themes consistently emerged:

If I had it to do over again, I would reflect more.
If I had it to do over again, I would risk more.
If I had it to do over again, I would do more things that would live on after I am dead.

When you come to the end of your life, I hope you have no regrets, that you have lived life to the fullest and done everything you can every day to make the most of your time on earth. Being intentional about your legacy and living it out every day will help you do that.

3. Appreciate Today the Value of a Good Legacy

Charles F. Kettering, inventor and onetime head of General Motors' research division, stated, "The greatest thing this generation can do is lay a few stepping stones for the next generation." There is great joy in taking others to places they have never been and to heights they have never dreamed possible. As a leader, you have a great opportunity to do those things.

Most people don't get to choose when or how they're going to die. But they can decide how they're going to live.

I think the ability to create a positive legacy is greatly dependent on a person's attitude. First, you must care about people. Second, you must appreciate how great an impact a good legacy can make. But you also have to have the right perspective. You must come to realize how unimportant you are in comparison to the task with which you have been entrusted as a leader. That requires a level of objectivity, maturity, and humility that many leaders never attain. Your goal as a leader isn't to be indispensable to the people you lead; it is to leave your people something that is indispensable to them.

Educator D. Elton Trueblood wrote, "We have made at least a start in discovering the meaning in human life when we plant shade trees under which we know full well we will never sit." That is the right kind of perspective for a legacy creator.

INVESTING IN THE NEXT GENERATION

I realize that my perspective on the subject of legacy is strongly influenced by my phase of life. I'm sixty years old, our children are grown, and Margaret and I are in the time of life when we are enjoying our grandchildren. In contrast, if you have a young family, your current focus for your legacy building is probably your children. That is as it should be. When our children were young, Margaret and I were focused on instilling values and skills in Elizabeth and Joel. As they were growing up, we determined that we wanted to give them four things:

- Unconditional love
- A foundation of faith
- Life/success principles
- Emotional security

I'm delighted to say that our children are now married, living their own lives, and passing their own values down to their children. And Margaret and I are seeing the values, hopes, dreams, experiences, and blessings of our family passed down to another generation. It is very rewarding, and it reminds me of something said by social reformer Henry Ward Beecher: "We should so live and labor in our time that what came to us as seed may go to the next generation as blossom; and what came to us as blossom may go to them as fruit. This is what we mean by progress."

> *"We have made at least a start in discovering the meaning in human life when we plant shade trees under which we know full well we will never sit."*
> —*D. Elton Trueblood*

There is a poem called "The Bridge Builder" that I have enjoyed for many years. It was written by Tennessee poet Will Allen Dromgoole, and describes what it means to create a legacy for those who follow us:

An old man, going a lone highway,
Came at the evening, cold and gray,
To chasm, vast and deep and wide,
Through which was flowing a sullen tide.
The old man crossed in the twilight dim;
The sullen stream had no fears for him;
But he turned when safe on the other side
And built a bridge to span the tide.

"Old man," said a fellow pilgrim near,
"You are wasting strength with building here;
Your journey will end with the ending day;
You never again must pass this way;
You have crossed the chasm, deep and wide—
Why build you the bridge at the eventide?"

The builder lifted his old gray head:
"Good friend, in the path I have come," he said,
"There followeth after me today
A youth whose feet must pass this way.
This chasm that has been naught to me
To that fair-haired youth may a pit-fall be,
He, too, must cross in the twilight dim;
Good friend, I am building the bridge for him."

What kind of a bridge are you building for those who follow behind you? Are you making the most of your leadership—not just for yourself, not just for those who follow you today, but also for those who will follow you tomorrow? Knowing that someday people will summarize your life in one sentence is sobering. Picking it now is a way of saying thank you to God, life, family, and others you will never meet.

PEOPLE WILL SUMMARIZE YOUR LIFE IN ONE SENTENCE—PICK IT NOW

APPLICATION EXERCISES

1. How important has a legacy been to you? For many leaders, leaving a legacy is the last thing on their minds. Where does it rate for you? Had you considered the idea before reading the chapter? Are you prepared to begin considering what you would like it to be? No matter where you are in the leadership journey—whether you are a young leader "wet behind the ears" or a "grizzled veteran," it's never too early to start thinking about what you want your life to mean to others when it's done. Choose to make the creation of a legacy a priority.

2. What do you want your legacy to be? Determining your legacy takes time. To start the process, ask yourself the following three questions:

- What are my responsibilities? (This helps identify what you *should* do.)
- What are my abilities? (This helps identify what you *can* do.)
- What are my opportunities? (This helps identify what you *could* do.)

After answering the questions, try to use your answers to write a succinct "life sentence."

3. Are you living that legacy today? A legacy does not get created simply because a person writes down a life sentence. It happens because the person lives it out every day. Does your current life conform to the life sentence you have written for yourself? If not, why? What must you stop doing? What must you start doing? What must you do more of? The adjustments to your life may be small or may require making major transitions. Start working on them today.

MENTORING MOMENT

Ask the people you're mentoring to identify the ultimate goal of their work. Ask them to describe what it will be like (and what *they* will be like) when they get there. Ask them to explain why they have chosen that goal and what it will take to get there. Get them to flesh it out as much as they can. Now ask them to describe in what ways their current actions consistently support their goal and in what ways their actions are inconsistent with or undermining their goal. Prompt them to identify the changes they need to make to put them on the right course for their goals. Ask them to write out a legacy statement followed by a list of values they must embrace and actions they must take to give them the best chance of achieving that legacy.

CONCLUSION

I hope you have enjoyed the twenty-six gold nuggets that I included in this book. More importantly, I hope you have benefited from them. The danger with a book like this is that it's easy to breeze through it, understanding the concepts that are contained in it but not actually *doing* anything with them. Information alone will not help you become a better leader. You need to apply it to your life if you want to change and become better.

If leadership is new to you, then I trust that you are already seeing improvements in your leadership ability as a result of reading this book and learning from my mistakes. Whatever you do, don't stop there. Leadership doesn't develop in a moment. It develops over a lifetime, and the more intentional you are about your leadership growth, the greater your potential for becoming the leader you're capable of being. Never stop learning.

If you are a seasoned, successful leader and many of the things in this book are merely a reminder of what you already know, then put your focus where it should be: on raising up other leaders. Never forget that your greatest potential value isn't in your leadership; it's in your ability to take people with leadership potential and help them become successful leaders. You can make a greater impact by developing a small cadre of leaders than by leading a huge army of followers.

And no matter where you are in the leadership journey, keep growing, keep leading, and keep working to make a difference.

NOTES

Chapter 2

1. "We Have Met the Enemy . . . and He Is Us,"
   http://www.igopogo.com/we_have_met.htm, accessed 18 January 2007.
2. Proverbs 22:7 (NIV).

Chapter 3

1. F. John Reh, "Employee Benefits as a Management Tool,"
   http://management.about.com/cs/people/a/Benefits100198.htm, accessed 10 July 2007.

Chapter 5

1. Mark Albion, *Making a Life, Making a Living: Reclaiming Your Purpose and Passion in Business and Life* (New York: Warner Books, 2000), 17.

Chapter 6

1. Jim Lange, *Bleedership* (Mustang, OK: Tate, 2005), 76.
2. Lorin Woolfe, *The Bible on Leadership: From Moses to Matthew—Management Lessons for Contemporary Leaders* (New York: AMACOM, 2002), 103–4.

Chapter 7

1. Marcus Buckingham and Donald O. Clifton, *Now Discover Your Strengths* (New York: The Free Press, 2001), 6.

Chapter 8

1. Peter Drucker, *Managing in Turbulent Times* (New York: Harper Collins, 1980), 6.
2. Jim Collins, *Good to Great* (New York: Harper Collins, 2001), 70.

Chapter 9

1. Second presidential debate with incumbent Jimmy Carter, 28 October 1980, "Reagan in His Own Words," NPR, http://www.npr.org/news/specials/obits/reagan/audio_archive.html, accessed 19 February 2007.
2. Stuart Briscoe, *Everyday Discipleship for Ordinary People* (Wheaton, IL: Victor Books, 1988), 28.

Chapter 11

1. Barry Conchie, "The Seven Demands of Leadership: What Separates Great Leaders from All the Rest," *Gallup Management Journal*, 13 May 2004, http://gmj.gallup.com/content/11614/Seven-Demands-Leadership.aspx.

2. Stan Toler and Larry Gilbert, *Pastor's Playbook: Coaching Your Team for Ministry* (Kansas City: Beacon Hill Press, 1999).

Chapter 12
1. Michael Abrashoff, *It's Your Ship: Management Techniques from the Best Damn Ship in the Navy* (New York: Warner Business, 2002), 33.
2. Ibid., 91–92.

Chapter 13
1. Warren G. Bennis, *Managing the Dream: Reflections on Leadership and Change* (New York: Perseus Books, 2000), 56–57.
2. Jeffrey Davis, *A Thousand Marbles* (Kansas City, MO: Andrews McMeel, 2001).

Chapter 16
1. Malcolm Gladwell, *Blink: The Power of Thinking Without Thinking* (New York: Little, Brown, and Company, 2005), 18–34.
2. "Trust a Bust at U.S. Companies; Manchester Consulting's Survey Rates Trust in the Work Place a 5-1/2 Out of 10," http://www.prnewswire.com/cgi-bin/stories.pl?ACCT=104&STORY=/www/story/9-2-97/308712&EDATE=, accessed 27 March 2007.

Chapter 17
1. Harry Golden, *The Right Time: An Autobiography* (New York: Putnam, 1969).

Chapter 18
1. Harry Chapman, *Greater Kansas City Medical Bulletin* 63, http://www.bartleby.com/63/17/4517.html, accessed 9 March 2007.

Chapter 21
1. Proverbs 29:2 (MSG).

Chapter 23
1. *Reader's Digest*, 13 July 2003, 198.

Chapter 24
1. Dan Sullivan and Catherine Nomura, *The Laws of Lifetime Growth: Always Make Your Future Bigger Than Your Past* (San Francisco: Berrett-Koehler, 2006), 43.

Chapter 25
1. Matthew 16:26 (NIV).

BOOKS BY DR. JOHN C. MAXWELL
CAN TEACH YOU HOW TO BE A REAL SUCCESS

RELATIONSHIPS

Be a People Person

Becoming a Person of Influence

Relationships 101

The Power of Influence

The Power of Partnership in the Church

The Treasure of a Friend

Ethics 101

Winning with People

25 Ways to Win with People

EQUIPPING

Developing the Leaders Around You

Equipping 101

The 17 Indisputable Laws of Teamwork

The 17 Essential Qualities of a Team Player

Partners in Prayer

Your Road Map for Success

Success One Day at a Time

Today Matters

Talent Is Never Enough

ATTITUDE

Be All You Can Be

Failing Forward

The Power of Thinking Big

Living at the Next Level

Think on These Things

The Winning Attitude

Your Bridge to a Better Future

The Power of Attitude

Attitude 101

Thinking for a Change

The Difference Maker

The Journey from Success to Significance

LEADERSHIP

The 21 Indispensable Qualities of a Leader

Revised & Updated 10th Anniversary Edition of *The 21 Irrefutable Laws of Leadership*

The 21 Most Powerful Minutes in a Leader's Day

Developing the Leader Within You

Leadership 101

Leadership Promises for Every Day

The 360 Degree Leader

The Right to Lead

The Power of Leadership

Leadership Gold

Go for Gold

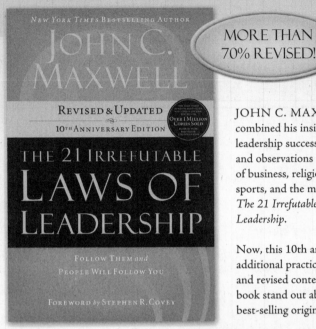
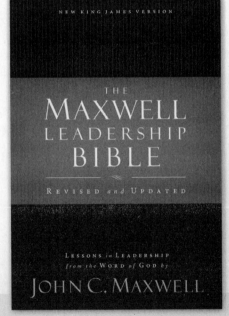